POWER OF THE CROSS

To Mary
Warmly,
Mary P. Halleck, Ed.D

March 2010

POWER OF THE CROSS

Mary Paloumpis Hallick, EdD

Holy Cross Orthodox Press
Brookline, Massachusetts

Publication of this book has been made possible in part by a generous contribution from Marian and Spyros Catechis In honor and memory of Anastasios Spero Catechis

Published by
Holy Cross Orthodox Press
50 Goddard Avenue
Brookline, Massachusetts 02445

ISBN 978-1-935317-02-9

Library of Congress Cataloging-in-Publication Data

Hallick, Mary P.
Power of the cross / Mary Paloumpis Hallick.
p. cm.
Includes bibliographical references (p.).
ISBN 978-1-935317-02-9 (alk. paper)
1. Crosses. 2. Holy Cross. 3. Orthodox Eastern Church. I. Title.
BV160.H36 2009
246′.558--dc22   2008046030

Printed in China by Sun Fung Offset Binding Co.,Ltd.

For
Thana and Connie
My critics, my friends, and my daughters

Contents

ACKNOWLEDGMENTS

A wise man said, "I alone can do it, but I can't do it alone." This book could not have been written without the advice and encouragement of many.

To the dear people who patiently read the manuscript in all its numerous drafts, my heartfelt thanks to you, Harriet Sporaa, Helen Canelos, Thana Moore, and Melissa Ramskugler. Your comments and suggestions were invaluable.

For the generosity of Dr. Jordan Lewis, Rabbi Brickman, Dr. Ninette Nassif, Fr. Ev. Constantinides, Deacon Vasilije Vranic, Fr. John Brown, and the librarians in Germantown, Wisconsin, who supplied valuable information, I am grateful.

Mike Christopoulos played a critical and integral role in bringing the manuscript together. His expertise is greatly appreciated.

Without Katherine de Shazer's artwork, this would be nothing more than a thousand words.

My granddaughters, Tiffany and Stephanie, the computer gurus, helped immensely.

And to my daughters, Connie and Thana, and my brother, Herc, thank you for your positive and negative comments, but above all, for your encouragement to continue.

Mary Paloumpis Hallick, EdD

Chapter 1

THE CROSS IN EARLY CHRISTIANITY

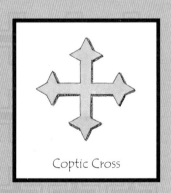

Coptic Cross

Today, the cross is everywhere we look: dangling on necklaces, stitched to firefighters' jackets, painted on ambulances, and reaching for the sky atop church steeples and domes. It's the most familiar sign of Christianity, and when we see it, we remember Jesus Christ and his Resurrection. But the early Christians saw the cross as a symbol of shame and dishonor because their Lord and Savior was crucified on it as a common criminal. The cross had been used for untold centuries as a means of execution. Therefore, for early Christians the cross was not a symbol of their faith but rather a remembrance of the disgrace and humiliation that Jesus suffered.

Instead of focusing on the way Jesus died, early Christians emphasized his gift of salvation by celebrating the Eucharist—sharing the gifts of Jesus's body and blood in communion. They regularly gathered together in an *ecclesia* (assembly), usually a private home, for prayer, worship, a remembrance of the Last Supper, learning, and fellowship. The emphasis of the Eucharist was on the ritual, signifying the sacrificial death of Christ. Strange as it may seem, archaeological digs from cemeteries used prior to the third century did not show any symbols or figures suggesting the importance of the suffering and death of Jesus Christ. The cross did not appear in any of the archaeological findings.

Christians had other figures to show that they were followers of Christ. Examples of these religious drawings are found in the catacombs (underground burial places) in Rome, first discovered in 1578. (All dates are AD unless otherwise noted.) The catacombs extended for great distances under the earth. For centuries, the Romans had used land above ground for their cemeteries, but over time the land on the surface became filled. The people began to dig out caves under the graves to create another level for burying bodies—and then they dug another level deeper once the first one was full. Eventually the cemeteries went down several levels. From these catacombs, we learn of the various symbols early Christians used.

The catacombs had hollowed out places in the walls for the tombs and sarcophagi of departed loved ones as well as semicircular areas where the relatives and friends would gather to worship. Not only were the tombs decorated, but the walls of the catacombs were also decorated. The Romans painted pictures of plants, birds, fish, and letters of the Greek alphabet throughout the catacombs, creating a network of galleries.

In the first two centuries of Christianity, sketches in the catacombs were not ornate. The palm frond and palm tree were popular forms found on the tombs and sarcophagi. Even though the palm was a pagan symbol of victory, early Christians chose it to signify the victory of people who died for Christ: the saints and martyrs. In Revelation 7:9 we read, "They would appear before the Lamb [Christ] clothed in white robes and palms in their hands."

Another symbol popular with early Christians was the dove, which represented purity and peace. It recalled for the faithful the story of the flood, when Noah sent out a dove and it returned with an olive branch to show him that the flood was over. Also, the dove was the form that the Holy Spirit took as he came down from heaven during the baptism of Jesus.

The symbol of the phoenix was introduced into Christianity as early as the first century. According to legend, this bird lived in the Arabian wilderness and lived between 300 and 500 years. When the phoenix neared the end of its life, it would burn itself on a funeral pyre and then rise from its ashes to begin another life cycle. Early Christians used this symbol to show the life and resurrection of Christ.

Some symbols came from the Greek language, such as *icthys* (ΙΧΘΥΣ), the Greek word for fish. Christians used this word as an acronym of *Isous, Christos, Theou, Yion, Soter*: "Jesus Christ, Son of God, Savior." The Greek letters alpha and omega (A and Ω) were also popular Christian symbols inscribed on the walls of the Roman catacombs. The Lord said, "I am the Alpha and the Omega, the Beginning and the End" (Rev 1:8). Other biblical imagery painted on the walls of the catacombs included symbols of Christ, people in prayer, and scenes from the Old Testament. The figure of a lamb appeared as a symbol of Christ—the *Lamb of God* (John 1:29)—who is the sacrificed victim for the sins of humankind, but Christ also was depicted as the good shepherd (John 10:11–18). Paintings of Christ as the vine recall His words in John 15:1, "I am the true vine." Scenes from the Old Testament, such as Daniel in the fiery furnace, Noah and the ark, and Jonah and the whale, were found on the walls. In all of these symbols and the vastness of the catacombs, the cross was not present.

Immediately following Christ's crucifixion, His followers carried on His teachings. They lived together in small, self-contained communities, but Paul and his disciples went out into a hostile environment to preach the teachings of Jesus. St. Paul preached that the crucifixion was fundamental to salvation. He said that "being crucified with Christ" (Gal 2:20) was an unspoken recognition of the faith. Paul taught that salvation was through the cross. A mass conversion of pagans to Christianity began in southern Europe and Asia Minor, and these new Christians came from all classes of society.

Even though the cross as a symbol was not prevalent, Christians were making the sign of the cross on their bodies. (This will be discussed in Chapter 5.) They were using the sign of the cross to identify themselves as Christians and to ward off the power of demons. This is not mentioned in the New Testament, but the practice of making the sign of the cross was widespread and everyone took the custom for granted.

Tertullian (ca. 160–230), a Latin theologian, was the first to use Latin instead of Greek in his theological writings. He noticed the common practice of Christians making the sign of the cross on their foreheads and wrote, "At every coming in and going out, in putting on our clothes and our shoes, in bath, at table lying down or sitting, we mark our foreheads with a little sign of the cross."

Others commented about the sign of the cross, including Andreopolous, who cites St. Cyril of Jerusalem. In the fourth century, St. Cyril wrote:

> Let us then not be ashamed to confess the Crucified. Let the cross be our seal, be boldly made with our fingers upon our brow and on all occasions; over the bread we eat; over the cups we drink; in our comings and our goings; before we sleep; on lying down and rising up; when we are on our way; and when we are still. It is a powerful safeguard; it is without price; for the sake of the poor; without toil, because of the sick; for it is a grace from God, a badge of the faithful, and a terror to the devils; for "he displayed them openly, leading them in a way of triumph by the force of it." For when they see the Cross, they are reminded of the Crucified; they fear him who has "smashed the heads of the dragons." Despise not the seal as a free gift, but rather for this reason honor your benefactor all the more.

Although individual Christians erected outdoor crosses, the cross was not generally used until the later part of the third century. In those first centuries, symbols known only to fellow Christians were best because the political climate, at times, was very unkind to the Christians. Periodically, there were mass persecutions of Christians. Under Nero (54–68), the Christians were blamed for burning Rome. During the reigns of Trajanus Decius (98–117) and Diocletian (284–305), Christians anywhere in the Empire were liable to be put to death, and the destruction of all Christian churches and the religion was ordered. Christians, who refused to publicly sacrifice to the pagan gods, were considered a danger to the Empire, and they were executed.

Although Christians were a minority, they were causing a disturbance throughout the Roman Empire. The national feeling was that the pagan religion was what made Rome great. The people felt that Christianity undermined the devotion to their gods and thus threatened the strength and power of the Roman state. As a result, there was a renewal in paganism. However, Christianity persisted in competing with the pagan religion.

Not only were the Christians persecuted, but they were also harassed and ridiculed. A famous bit of graffiti appears on the walls of a building on the Palatine Hill of Rome. (The Palatine Hill was the central of the seven hills on which Rome was built. The other hills were Capitoline, Quirinal, Viminal, Esquiline, Caelian, and Aventine.) This blasphemous caricature of Christ's crucifixion shows two men, one on a cross and the other possibly worshipping the figure on the cross. However, the figure on the cross has the head of a donkey. Under the drawing is the inscription written in Greek, "Alexamenos worships his god." This graffiti seems to depict a pagan servant ridiculing his fellow servant.

Early Christianity was growing slowly, but it had many obstacles to overcome. This new religion was in competition with paganism, and the followers of Christ refused to sacrifice to the pagan gods. They were blamed for many catastrophes that occurred, such as famine, drought, disease, and economic depression. The early Christians stood fast and did not bow down to the pagan emperors.

"I am the Alpha and the Omega,"
says the Lord God, "who is and who was
and who is to come, the Almighty."

Revelation 1:8

Chapter 2

CONSTANTINE THE GREAT & THE CROSS

Chi-Rho Cross

As the ruler of the Roman Empire, Constantine had a great impact on the Western world. He changed the society's beliefs, its values, and how it would act toward all people. He paved the way for Christianity to merge with the traditions of the Greco-Roman world. Under Constantine's social and economic regime, Christian art and literature developed. Above all, with his guidance, Church leaders defined Christian dogma and set up guidelines for leading a Christian life.

This great man, Constantine, the son of Constantius Chlorus and Helena, was born at Naissus (present-day Niš, Serbia) in 280. He lived in the eastern part of the Roman Empire and received his military training in Emperor Diocletian's court. Constantine spoke both Greek and Latin and showed a great interest in the religious supernatural.

Constantine served in the army and held many military ranks. When his father died in 306, Constantine was hailed as the successor by his father's troops, who gave him the title Augustus of the Western Empire. Maximian, who was already Augustus of the Western Empire, did not accept the fact that Constantine was replacing him. Consequently, Constantine and Maximian met in battle at Marseilles in 310, and Constantine was victorious.

To become the Roman Empire's sole ruler, Constantine next had to fight Maxentius. Maxentius, the son of Maximian, did not like Constantine—especially after Maximian fell in battle to Constantine. Maxentius was also very jealous of Constantine's success. Inevitably, they met in a fateful battle on October 28, 312, at the Milvian Bridge. This strategic bridge crossed the Tiber River about two miles from Rome.

The evening before the battle, Constantine saw a cross in the sky with these words: "in this sign conquer." In Greek, this phrase is εν τούτο νίκα (*en touto nika*); it is rendered in Latin as *in hoc signo vinces*. Constantine ordered his troops to place the image of this cross— which was formed by the first two letters of the word "Christ" in Greek, *chi* (X) and *rho* (P)—on their armor. The troops were exhausted from fighting, but they obeyed Constantine. They painted the cross on their shields, rallied, and won the battle. Once Maxentius saw that he was losing, he retreated across the bridge. In his haste for safety, Maxentius fell into the Tiber River and drowned.

The eagle had been the emblem of the Romans for many centuries, appearing on all their flags and banners. But once Constantine had seen the cross in the sky and was victorious, he ordered his subjects to remove the eagle symbol from the banners and replaced it with the chi-rho cross. Known as the Labarum, Constantine's insignia marked the beginning of the positive acceptance of the cross as a religious symbol of Christianity.

In 313, Constantine invited Licinius, who was the emperor of the Roman Empire in the east, to meet him in Milan. Their meeting and discussions produced the Edict of Milan, an important document giving Christians their religious freedom. The famous declaration granted Christians and Jews the freedom to practice their religions without fear of punishment by the Roman government. Unfortunately, Constantine has not been given appropriate recognition for this achievement.

Constantine was the first emperor to declare religious freedom for all people. He set aside Sunday as a public holiday and as a day of worship, and he decreed that slaves and freedmen who committed the same type of crime would receive the same kind of punishment. In addition, Constantine ordered that all men who had been banished to work in galleys or mines be recalled and given their freedom and their confiscated properties restored. He also gave special privileges to the clergy by relieving them of paying taxes.

These were all important advances in law, but the most important change that Constantine made was to outlaw execution by crucifixion. Constantine felt that Christ's crucifixion was an embarrassment: God's own Son was subjected to such humiliation. For this reason, Constantine abolished crucifixion as a punishment, removing the stigma of shame and humiliation that the cross represented.

The decrees of the Edict of Milan were made with good intentions, but Licinius, in the eastern part of the Roman Empire, stopped short of putting the changes into effect. Licinius still worshipped pagan gods, and he suddenly realized that the Edict of Milan made Christianity the preferred religion of the Roman Empire. He began removing Christians from his civil service ranks.

When Constantine learned of this, he declared war on Licinius. After a decade of disagreements and on-and-off fighting, the decisive battle between Constantine and Licinius took place on July 23, 324, at Chrysopolis (formerly Scutari; now known as Üsküdar, Turkey), a city across the Bosporus from Constantinople. Constantine prevailed, becoming the sole ruler of the Roman Empire.

In the beginning of the fourth century, less than ten percent of the population of the Roman Empire was Christian. By the time Constantine became the sole ruler of the empire, the Christian population was growing rapidly. By the end of the century, more than half the population were followers of Christ.

In spite of the progress that Christians were making, Constantine's new religion was not unified. Arius (250–336), a priest in Alexandria, Egypt, was teaching that Jesus was one of God's creations.

He taught that even though Jesus was divine, he was made of a different substance than the Father, was not eternal, and had not always existed. This teaching by Arius threatened the character of the Holy Trinity. Bishops, priests, and laypeople hotly debated this issue, which became known as the Arian Controversy. Athanasius, bishop of Alexandria, spoke out against this thinking. Thus Athanasius and Arius were in dire conflict and became enemies.

Constantine felt this controversy would disrupt the peace in his empire. Constantine was a man of order and discipline, and he could not have a religion that was in conflict. Believing it was his moral and ethical obligation to intervene to settle the dispute, he sent a letter to both Athanasius and Arius asking—rather, pleading—with them to come to a compromise. This did not happen.

In 325, Constantine confirmed his authority as sole ruler of the empire by calling all the bishops to convene and settle the controversy affecting Christianity. He assembled the First Ecumenical Council of the Church at the city of Nicaea, in Bithynia. (Interestingly, Nicaea was named for Nike, the goddess of victory.) Some historians contend that he picked Nicaea so that he could attend the council meeting while overseeing construction of his new city, Constantinople, which was being built on the old Greek city of Byzantium.

Constantine viewed this meeting as very important. He desired the council to be well attended, so he paid all of the travel expenses for the 318 bishops, priests, deacons, and theologians who attended. To ensure that they would be comfortable, all council members were housed in his palaces. The members of the council came from all parts of the empire. According to reports, one delegate came from Cordoba, Spain. Another delegate, Sylvester, traveled from Rome, and Alexander and Athanasius came from Alexandria, Egypt, to participate in the debates.

The council, in its lengthy deliberations, affirmed that the Father and the Son were equal, the same in essence, eternity, and divinity. The Fathers used the Greek term *homoousios* (identical substance) to describe the relationship between God and Jesus. This term was deliberately used to reject Arius, who was found at fault and exiled. Findings and deliberations of this council not only became the law of the Church but also law of the land.

Constantine built his city, New Rome or Constantinople, and erected many churches there. Pleased with the outcome of the First Ecumenical Council, Constantine wanted to give thanks to God. In appreciation, he authorized the erection of a basilica built on the place where Christ was buried. In 327, he chose his mother, Helena Augusta, to accomplish this task.

There is much conjecture about Helena and her life. She was a devout Christian, but when did she become a Christian? Some say she came to the faith while she was still a young girl living in York, England. Others say she accepted Christianity only after her son Constantine saw the chi-rho cross in the heavens before the battle at the Milvian Bridge.

Helena was born around 248, and her place of birth has not been determined. Some historians say she was born in Bithynia. Some report that she was a stabularia (a bar maid, a landlady of a tavern, or an owner of a great house). The chronicler Geoffrey of Monmouth (d. 1154) gives her a greater status, saying she was the daughter of King Coel of Colchester (as in "Old King Cole was a merry old soul"). Some writers criticized Helena, but she rose to a place of eminence as she aged. While Constantine was in York, England, he made his mother dowager empress. She was given the honorific title of Augusta, and she maintained this title all her life.

Constantine asked his mother to undertake the long and dangerous journey to Aelia Capitolina (the Roman name for Jerusalem). Again, historians differ as to why she accepted this mission but agree that she eagerly accepted the assignment. Most likely, Helena was in her late seventies or early eighties when she began her journey. She did not travel alone. Constantine not only had an entourage of servants accompany her, but he also provided an army to protect her and her attendants through this long and dangerous journey.

In addition to her royal entourage, Eusebius (ca. 260–339), the bishop of Caesarea, accompanied Helena. Eusebius, who is called the Father of Church History, wrote that she visited soldiers, gave them bonuses, and gave money to the poor. Everywhere she went she talked about Constantine's benevolence and of Christianity.

Upon arriving in Jerusalem, Helena began her quest for Christ's tomb. She was informed that, according to custom, the crosses of those who had been crucified were buried in a deep ditch and then covered with dirt and stones. Where would she find the Holy Cross to erect the basilica that her son wanted?

To add to the dilemma, at the time of Christ's crucifixion the Romans did not want the Christians to find the location of Christ's burial place and therefore went to great lengths to conceal it.

The exact location was not generally known to the people, but it was common knowledge in Jerusalem that a Hebrew family was entrusted with this secret. The information was handed down from one generation to the next. A relative of the family, an old man, was located. He did not want to divulge the secret, but after much persuasion he disclosed the place.

Christ had been crucified on the site where the temple to Venus had been erected. When Emperor Hadrian reconstructed Jerusalem as Aelia Capitolina in 135, he built temples to the pagan gods of Greece and Rome. He erected a temple to the goddess of Venus on the site of the crucifixion of Jesus as a pagan protest against Christianity.

Tradition states that Helena had the temple torn down and was then able to identify the precise spot when she noticed a profusion of the sweet basil plant. After much excavation three crosses were found along with the nails. Theodoret of Cyrus (d. ca. 457) wrote in his *Ecclesiastical History* that when the tomb was discovered, there were three crosses nearby. Certain that the crosses were those of Jesus Christ and the two thieves who were crucified with Him, but unable to tell which was the true Cross, Makarios, bishop of the city, settled the problem. A woman who had been suffering from disease was brought to the site, and each cross was brought to her. The instant the true Cross was brought near her, she was cured of the disease.

Helena immediately sent word to Constantine that she had found the true Cross. A series of flaming torches transmitted the news from one signal tower to another along the prominent headlands along the coast of the eastern Mediterranean Sea until it reached Constantinople. Helena sent a piece of the Holy Cross and the nails to her son in his capital.

The Church of the Holy Resurrection that Helena constructed on the site was completed in 335. While in the Holy Land, Helen oversaw the building of many churches. In addition to the Church of the Holy Resurrection, Helena built the Church of the Nativity in Bethlehem, a church at Mamre, and a church referred to as the Eleon on the Mount of Olives at the traditional site of Jesus's ascension to heaven.

The finding of the true Cross and the construction of churches on the historical sites thrilled the Christians. Many visitors came to the once-quiet place of Jerusalem. Visitors from all parts of Europe traveled to Jerusalem to walk on the land that Jesus walked and visit the places of their Savior.

An eleventh-century manuscript, which was found in 1884 and validated as authentic in 1903, told of a visit of a nun who came from northwestern Spain and traveled to Egypt, the Holy Land, Edessa, and Constantinople. The title of her letter was *Itinerium Egeriae* (Egeria's Travels). Her journey began in 381 and lasted three years.

Egeria sent a long letter to her fellow nuns describing shrines and places identified with the life, death, resurrection, and ascension of Christ. She told them of the various religious services she attended in Jerusalem, such as the Feast of Epiphany, Holy Week and Easter, the Veneration of the Cross, and Pentecost. The letter she sent back to the convent encouraged pilgrims to travel from far away to see the holy places. Within a short time, Jerusalem became a Christian tourist attraction.

Christianity flourished under Constantine's rule, yet some historians stressed the negative points of his life and questioned his Christian faith. Constantine was degraded for waiting almost until his dying day to be baptized, but there were valid reasons why Constantine delayed his baptism.

In accordance with the custom of his day, Constantine postponed his baptism until he was near death. Constantine feared and respected God. He deeply believed that the Christian God was a God of power, and Constantine felt that God had given him power to be victorious. Believing in divine anger, Constantine delayed baptism so that he would not endanger his soul.

Constantine had also hoped to travel to the Holy Land to be baptized in the Jordan River but was not accorded his desire. Constantine died on May 21, 339.

Before Constantine, the cross did not carry religious or symbolic significance. Its status changed with Constantine. No longer looked upon with shame and humiliation, the cross became a symbol to be honored and revered. Constantine and his mother Helena made this possible. Constantine gave the Christian faith strength, and Helena helped by traveling to far places to promote Christianity. Using finances from the imperial treasury, Helena built several churches at historic places in Jerusalem. For these pious works and the spreading of Christianity, Constantine and Helena were declared "equal to the apostles" by the Orthodox Church. They are commemorated on the same feast day, May 21, in the Orthodox Church.

εν τούτο νίκα
by this sign conquer

Chapter 3

THE HOLY CROSS & ITS EVOLUTION

Greek Cross

During the first two centuries of Christianity, the cross was not in widespread use as a symbol for the faith, but its popularity grew when Constantine declared religious freedom for pagans, Christians, and Jews. With Constantine's conversion, there was explosive growth in the use of the cross. Popular forms were the Greek cross, the Latin cross, and the tau cross. The cross with arms of equal length is the Greek cross; in the Latin cross, the vertical arm is longer than the horizontal arm; and the tau cross is the shape of the Greek letter T. Over time, the crosses became elaborately crafted and ornately decorated.

The cross symbol was being accepted and openly displayed. Early Greek manuscripts give us information about the common use of the cross. One manuscript informs us that when the members of the First Ecumenical Council in 325 presented their credentials to Constantine, Greek crosses adorned their robes. Other records indicate that in 461, St. Hilarius was the first prelate to wear a pectoral cross. St. Hilarius was a disciple of St. Anthony, the father of monasticism.

Christians began inscribing crosses in catacombs at the end of the second century. Truly, these were rather primitive and crude, but by the fourth century, the crosses were becoming very ornate. Mosaic seemed to be the preferred medium for constructing the crosses. A fourth-century church at Ravenna, Italy, provides an excellent example of the use of mosaics. At the top of the azure dome is a large golden cross surrounded by gold stars. In the center of the cross is the head of Christ. (This mosaic icon is replicated in the apse of Saints Constantine and Helen Greek Orthodox Church, Wauwatosa, Wisconsin.)

The cross soon overshadowed all other symbols of Christianity. It was a simple design easily recognized by all. Artisans were creating crosses in all sizes, which they elaborately decorated and adorned with jewels. Jewels were significant in the design of the cross. Red stones, such as rubies and garnets, represented the blood of Christ. Green stones, like beryl and jade, denoted spiritual rebirth. The whiteness of pearls symbolized purity. Crosses were of a significant size and were used in both churches and homes.

One such ornate cross that still exists is a reliquary known as the Vatican Cross, which was given to Pope John III around 570. (A reliquary cross contains a relic of a saint.) This cross, a gift from Emperor Justin and his wife Sophia, was said to contain a relic of the true Cross. In the center of the reliquary cross is a medallion with the image of a lamb. At both ends of the vertical arm are two images of Christ *Pantocrator* (Ruler of All, Almighty). The horizontal arms of the cross have the image of Justin on one end and Sophia on the other end. The raised silverwork of the cross is studded with gems. Both Justin and Sophia have their palms extended in a gesture of prayer, showing that the earthly rulers are giving tribute to Christ the Judge and Pantocrator.

In addition to the crosses executed in silver, gold, and jewels, exquisitely carved ivory crosses were made in Alexandria, Egypt. An example of this appears on a quintych (a five-paneled screen). On the central panel Christ appears without a beard, a tradition of early Christian art. Another Alexandrian sixth-century ivory diptych shows an enthroned, bearded Christ with Saints Peter and Paul on either side.

Thanks to examples of old crosses and crucifixes from ancient frescoes and paintings, we have another source of knowledge about the history of the crosses. The Christians of the first few centuries often placed an image of a lamb or the bust of a youth above the cross to symbolize Jesus. These crosses did not show the body of Christ. Christianity in its early stages still followed some Jewish customs. The Jewish religion prohibited the use of images, considering it idolatrous. Furthermore, for early Christians the empty cross symbolized the resurrected Jesus, not the crucified Jesus.

By the fifth century, the body of the crucified Christ was added to the cross, creating the first crucifix. The crucifix cross then evolved. At first, only the head of Christ was shown, painted at either the top or the bottom of the cross. At the intersection of the arms, in the middle of the cross, a sacrificial lamb was painted.

The cross was appearing in iconography by the sixth century. An icon at the Monastery of St. Catherine at Mount Sinai depicts the head and bust of Christ. Christ is blessing with his right hand, and his left hand holds the Gospel, which is adorned with a jewel-studded cross. Justinian was the first monarch of the Byzantine Empire to have a cross on his crown, and he may have been the first to view the cross as a symbol of eternal life. His faith in the cross was so great that he was the first to build a church in the shape of the cross.

Crosses of the seventh century began depicting the entire figure of Christ either painted or carved on the cross. The figure of Christ in three dimensions appeared in the eighth century. At first, Christ was depicted as a young man, alive. He had no beard and there was no indication of wounds on his body, nor was there a crown of thorns on his head.

By the tenth century, the crucifix depicted Christ as dying or dead with an expression of suffering on his face. The body of Christ was covered from the neck to the knees. Crucifixes with the loincloth on the body of Christ did not appear until the fourteenth century.

The crucifix is used in the Orthodox Church, but it is not the same type of crucifix used in the Roman Catholic or some Protestant Churches. In those traditions, a three-dimensional body of Christ is depicted. Christ is shown as still suffering on the cross.

The crucifix of the Orthodox Church shows the body of Christ either painted or inscribed on the cross, and it depicts him as already dead. To the Orthodox Christian, the crucified Christ not only represents the suffering and agony of Christ, but it also exemplifies Christ the victor over death. The crucifixion, to the Orthodox Christian, denotes an act of victory over evil.

The Seventh Ecumenical Council, held at Nicaea in 787 during the reign of Constantine V and his mother Irene, defined the pictorial representation of the cross. In Act 7 of the council, we read,

> We define the rule with all accuracy and diligence, in a manner not unlike that befitting the shape of the precious and vivifying Cross, that the venerable and the holy icons painted on mosaic or made of any other suitable material be placed in the holy churches of God, upon sacred vessels, and vestments, walls, and panels, houses, and streets, both of our Lord and God and our Savior Jesus Christ.

The act does not mention a three-dimensional body of Christ on the crucifix.

The council wrote this act during a period of turmoil in the Orthodox Church known as the iconoclast period (726–876). The iconoclasts were "icon smashers" who rejected the use of icons. They destroyed many icons during this period, and many devout Christians were exiled or lost their lives defending the holy images.

Although the iconoclasts opposed the use of icons, they preferred the cross and the crucifix, which reminded them of Constantine's vision at the Milvian Bridge. Moreover, they encouraged the use of specifically decorative representations of the cross in church apses. Of course, those crosses did not depict the crucified Christ.

Leo III (717–757) was the first Byzantine emperor to openly act against the icons. He ordered his bishops to destroy the holy images at the gates of his palace because he believed they were pagan idols. At the Chalke (Bronze) Gate, the entrance of his palace, Leo III removed the icon of Christ but replaced it with a cross.

By the sixth century people were beginning to abuse the cross, using it irreverently. Crosses were drawn in the dirt and placed on thresholds, and therefore people walked on the cross. Indiscriminate use of the cross caused great concern for pious Christians. In 691 respect for the Holy Cross was brought up in a council at Trullo, the imperial palace of Justinian. (The hall in the palace where the meeting was held had a dome. The word *trullo* means dome.)

Canon 73 addresses this problem, stating that the crosses be removed from flooring, lest "The symbol signifying the trophy of victory to us be desecrated by being trod upon by people walking over the ground. We therefore decree that henceforth those who make the sign of the cross or imprint of the cross on the ground shall be excommunicated."

An interpretation section of this canon reports that a certain pope (whose name was not given) had the habit of drawing a cross on the ground, then erasing it with his foot. Since his foot had etched the cross on the dirt, he would offer his foot to his audience to be kissed. The writer referred to this as an "unchristian act."

The Holy Cross is the greatest and most esteemed of all the Christian symbols, evolving from the depths of shame to the highest levels of glory. The crude crosses of the catacombs became the beautifully ornate and bejeweled crosses of the Christian world. The symbol rose from being trod on at thresholds to its highest glory on the apses and domes of churches where everyone could raise their eyes to observe it.

Through the centuries the ecumenical councils defined the cross and its status. The Seventh Ecumenical Council in 787 gave explicit instructions regarding the Holy Cross. In veneration and respect, the Holy Gospel ranks first, followed by the Holy Cross. As we give honor and adoration to the Holy Cross, we are reminded that the Cross of Jesus Christ has been our symbol of victory for nearly 2,000 years.

Let us hang [the cross] over our bed instead of a sword;
let us inscribe it upon our door instead of a bolt or bar;
let us surround our house with it instead of a wall.

St. John Chrysostom

Chapter 4

THE HOLY CROSS IN CONFLICT

Latin Cross

Through the efforts of emperors, clergy, and theologians who participated faithfully in the ecumenical councils, the Holy Cross finally gained respect in the Christian world, appearing everywhere. Priests and bishops placed crosses on their vestments. The clergy blessed congregations with a cross-like gesture. Even churches were shaped in the form of a cross.

The cross also played an important role in the daily life of the people. In the commercial and financial life of the empire, the cross was used at the signing of contracts. Merchants petitioned the Holy Spirit and then marked the contract with the sign of the cross. Illiterate persons made a sign of the cross in place of a signature. In the fourth century, there were coins of Constantine with the cross in the form of the Labarum inscribed on them. Later, in the sixth century, Emperor Justinian minted coins with a Greek cross, with arms that ended in a leaf shape. Emperor Phocas, in the seventh century, issued coins that had an orb above the cross, signifying the supremacy of the spiritual world over the temporal world.

Unfortunately, political and economic forces troubled the Byzantine Empire. The empire was harassed and threatened by innumerable enemies and problems over several centuries. The territories of the empire were in danger of foreign occupation, but in addition to (and perhaps even more than) seeking land, invading non-Christian armies sought the trophy of the true Cross.

Eurasian tribes advanced to the west looking for places to settle. In the early summer of 401, Alaric the Goth invaded Italy, and by September 408, Rome had fallen to him. The Lombards, a Germanic people, invaded Italy in 568, not to conquer it but rather looking for a place to settle.

For many years, the empire believed it was safe because the Danube River blocked invading tribes from advancing further. Eventually, the Danube ceased holding off invaders. In 587, the Avars, a people probably of Tartar origin, launched an invasion. They joined forces with the Slavs and crossed the banks of the Danube. The might of the Avars and Slavs overran the Balkans. The Avars eventually left, but the Slavs remained.

Parts of Italy and the Balkan area were not the only regions to experience problems of invasion and settlement. The Sassanids, a Persian dynasty, launched raids on the Byzantine Empire. The conflict between Constantinople and the Persian capital, Ctesiphon (near present-day Baghdad), centered on the Fertile Crescent—the Tigris and Euphrates valley. The conflict among Greeks, Persians, and the Roman Empire had begun.

Not only was there territorial controversy, but religious conflict also occurred within the Church. From the Third Ecumenical Council in Ephesus (431) to the conclusion of the Sixth Ecumenical Council in Constantinople (681), the Church was confronted with rivalry between Constantinople and Alexandria and disagreement concerning the nature of Christ.

The First Ecumenical Council (325) agreed on the items in the Nicene Creed that defined the Holy Trinity: one God, three persons. Its formal explanation of the two natures of Christ refuted heretical Arian teachings.

The Second Ecumenical Council (381) was called to define Christ's divinity and humanity. A cleric, Macedonius, was declaring that the Holy Spirit was constructed or created by the Son—blasphemy according to the teachings of the Church. The Council rejected his theory and rightfully returned the glorification and adoration of the Holy Trinity. The Arians, who also attended this council, tried to alter the doctrine of the Nicene Creed but were unsuccessful.

This council also decided the religious authority of cities. Rome ranked first for prestige, followed by Constantinople for influence, then Alexandria and Antioch. By the middle of the fifth century, Jerusalem was added for its importance as Christ's birthplace. The patriarchs of these five cities made up the powers of the Christian world.

At the Fourth Ecumenical Council, held at Chalcedon (451), the bishops agreed that Christ had two natures in one person. The bishops added a further definition: "one and same Son, perfect in Godhead and perfect in manhood, truly God and truly man." However, a faction that originated in Egypt, known as the Monophysites, dissented: they believed that the two natures of Christ were fused into one. Sadly, this disagreement about the nature of Christ has not been fully resolved even today.

Territorial conflicts persisted as the Persians attacked the Byzantine Empire on the eastern front. An Arab tribe from Yemen, the Ghassanids, had settled along the desert frontier of Syria. During his reign, Justinian had placed a special honor on the chieftain of the tribe. This tribe and the chieftain were responsible for the safety of the desert frontier.

The Ghassanids were sympathetic to the Monophysites. Authorities in Constantinople were concerned and distressed, fearing that the Monophysites were under the control of the Ghassanids. Eventually, Maurice, who ruled the empire from 582–602, removed the special honor from the Ghassanids. Not only were the Ghassanids inflamed, but this action also caused dissension in the Monophysite church. More importantly, this situation threatened the stability of the eastern boundaries of the empire.

Unfortunately, this was not the only unrest in the empire. In 541, the empire experienced the onslaught of the bubonic plague. The horrid disease and epidemic began in central Africa and arrived in

Constantinople by way of the Red Sea. The plague spread into the eastern Mediterranean to the Balkans, North Africa, and Italy. The historian Procopius wrote that as many as 10,000 people died every day in Constantinople. Procopius and Emperor Justinian survived the illness, but Empress Theodora succumbed.

Because of the epidemic, the city of Constantinople and the empire were reduced to about one-third of their original populations. This alone caused a financial disaster to the empire. The loss of taxpayers to support the state combined with the human misery were enough to paralyze the empire.

Other problems in the state included mutinies in the army and unrest by the citizens. Major conflicts in religious beliefs centered on the doctrine of the person of Christ. Everyone seemed to have an idea about the nature of Christ, and great debates took place everywhere.

Like any government, the Byzantine Empire had factions. Two political parties, known as the Blues and Greens, were led by governmental appointees. Some of their duties included maintaining the defensive walls around the city, acting as part of the local militia, and performing guard duty.

In all cities of the empire, the Blues tended to be the party of the big landowners and the aristocracy, whereas the Greens were trades people, workers, and civil servants. The Blues eventually became associated with religious orthodoxy and the Greens with Monophysitism.

The Blue and Green factions became organized, and their members began to appear in towns and cities of the empire. They tended to cause unrest. Surprisingly, these groups did not carry any religious affiliations but provided an outlet for youthful violence—and violence did occur.

With all of the unrest, Emperor Maurice was deposed and Phocas came into power. His regime did not last long, from 602 to 610. To say the least, the empire was in turmoil. Where small towns had grown up around the hub of Constantinople, they now became walled cities known as *kastra* fortresses. Walls were erected to protect the hub and small towns from the invaders. The Sassanids occupied much of Anatolia, and by now the Byzantine army had dwindled. Constantinople was vulnerable.

In 610, Heraclius was elected to save the empire from the inadequacies of Phocas. Heraclius marched into Constantinople in triumph. Patriarch Sergius (a member of the Blue faction) and the Green faction became allies of Heraclius. Heraclius made several important decisions that helped the empire regain its strength.

First, he gave soldiers grants of land, contingent on their military service. This gave the empire a well-trained army. Second, he restored taxes, forced loans to be repaid, and imposed fines for past corruptions. Heraclius knew that unless he established order at home, he could not fight the Persians of the Sassanid dynasty. As Heraclius attempted to rectify weaknesses in the empire, the Persians were on the march.

The Sassanids under King Chosroes took Antioch in 611 and Damascus in 613. Onward they marched, taking Jerusalem in 614. The battle in Jerusalem was horrendous. Churches were destroyed, and hardly a Christian was left alive. The Church of the Holy Sepulchre and other Christian shrines were burned to the ground. (The Church of the Holy Sepulchre was later rebuilt, in 626.) The true Cross and other relics dear to Christianity became the spoils of war. Knowing their value, the Persians took them to their capital of Ctesiphon. Chosroes went on to capture Egypt in 619.

This was a terrible blow to the empire. Egypt was a chief supplier of corn to the empire, and Egypt was now a Persian province. Within a short time, Copt, the language of Egypt, was replaced by Arabic, the language of the conqueror.

A brilliant general, Heraclius built up alliances with the Armenians and the Georgians. He had an understanding with the Khazars, who were an important group on the steppes. With these new alliances, Heraclius was now ready to fight the Persians. He won an important victory in 627 when he defeated the Sassanids and recovered the true Cross.

Heraclius returned to Constantinople in triumph with the true Cross. The city of Constantinople honored him with a great reception and a procession. With the true Cross in the lead, Heraclius followed, and then came four elephants—the first ever seen in Constantinople. The procession traveled through the streets of Constantinople to the Church of Holy Wisdom (Hagia Sophia). After a service of thanksgiving, the Cross was placed on the altar. There it remained until 631, when Heraclius returned it to its rightful place, the Church of the Holy Resurrection in Jerusalem.

The true Cross and the city of Jerusalem enjoyed a short period of tranquility. However, another disturbing problem confronted the Byzantine Empire and the Christian world: the rise of Islam. Within a few years, the city of Jerusalem was under the control of new Arab conquerors.

Mohammed, a prophet and religious leader in Mecca, had become the leader of Arab tribes. He preached a monotheist religion, proclaiming that the divine judgment was near, and all were to give up their many gods and submit to this new faith. Mohammed taught that his Islamic followers were the descendants of Abraham through his son Ishmael (whom Abraham had cast out into the desert) and that the Arabs would be masters of the Holy Land. Mohammed's message united the Arab tribes, and they believed they were the "new chosen people." Their battle cry was, "There is only one God, Allah, and Mohammed is his prophet."

The Prophet Mohammed died in 632, but his followers were militant. They sent a diplomatic delegation to Heraclius, declaring:

> God has given this land as an inheritance to our father Abraham and to his posterity after him. We are the children of Abraham. You have held our country long enough. Give it up peacefully, and we will not invade your country. If not, we will retake with interest what you have withheld from us.

Heraclius ignored this declaration. He raised an army of about 80,000 men to fight to save Jerusalem. The armies met in May 636. Initially the Christians were winning, but three months later, on August 20, a fierce sandstorm occurred. The Byzantine army was neither trained nor equipped to fight a desert storm. Blinded by the sand, they were annihilated by the Arabs. Jerusalem resisted, but in the autumn of 637, the Patriarch of Jerusalem agreed to surrender. In February 638, the Caliph Omar rode into the Holy City on a white camel.

After the defeat, Heraclius, now in poor health, slipped into the city of Jerusalem. He removed the true Cross from the Church of the Holy Sepulchre and returned it to Constantinople for safekeeping.

Once the true Cross was back in the hands of Christians, it had to be protected. Non-Christians would always consider the Cross a trophy of war. The true Cross was cut and divided among the five Patriarchates (Rome, Constantinople, Alexandria, Antioch, and Jerusalem), the Monastery of St. Catherine at Mount Sinai, and Mount Athos.

As early as 350, St. Cyril of Jerusalem wrote, "The whole world has since been filled with pieces of the wood cross." By the Middle Ages, many churches, monasteries, emperors, clergy, and laypeople claimed to possess fragments of the cross. One person said that it would have been possible to rebuild the entire city of Jerusalem with fragments of the true Cross.

Because the Cross had already been divided into several segments by the time of the Crusades, it could have only gone into battle for the Holy Lands in pieces. In 1099, the Crusaders found another piece of the true Cross in Jerusalem. Mounted on a large metal cross and decorated with gold and silver, it was housed at the Church of the Holy Resurrection. The Franks took this piece of the true Cross as their own, but in 1187 it was lost to the Muslim sultan Saladin in the Battle of Hattin. This piece of the true Cross has never been recovered.

The Crusades began with noble efforts to free the Holy Land from the Muslim conquerors. The Crusaders were deployed to rescue the Holy Land from the Muslim invasion, to secure the safety of trade and travel routes, and to stop the Muslim conquest in the West. Sadly, the Crusades quickly deteriorated into exercises of greed and corruption and became a movement to expand the political and commercial interests of the Franks and Venetians. The aim of the Crusades was not to recover the true Cross but to obtain territory for economic gains.

Christians venerate not only the simple symbol of the cross but also the protected relics of the true Cross found by St. Helena. Unfortunately, the true Cross became a trophy of war. The Cross, the most important Christian relic, was seized not only by the Muslims but also by Christians of the West. They took it as their own and removed it from its proper place, the Church of the Holy Resurrection.

Wisely, the true Cross was divided and sent to the five Patriarchates, St. Catherine's Monastery, and Mount Athos for safekeeping. Moreover, it afforded the future generations of the Christian world a relic of Christ's suffering on the Cross. Try as they could, the offenders could not destroy the true Cross. The Holy Cross, a symbol of Christian faith, is recognized by one quarter of the world's population today.

Behold the Cross: guardian of the whole world!
Behold the Cross: the beauty of the Church!
Behold the Cross: the strength of the leaders!
Behold the Cross: the support of the faithful!
Behold the Cross: the glory of the angels and
the wounding of demons.

*Exapostilarion from the Matins of the
Feast of the Exaltation of the Holy Cross
(a hymn dating to 335, at the consecration of the
Church of the Holy Resurrection in Jerusalem)*

Chapter 5

THE HOLY CROSS & THE ORTHODOX CHRISTIAN

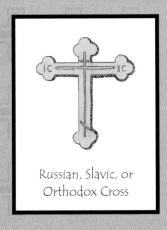

Russian, Slavic, or Orthodox Cross

The most important feast in the Christian faith is Pascha (Easter), the Feast of Feasts, which celebrates God's victory over death. The Orthodox Church stresses the resurrection of Christ and emphasizes apostolic preaching. However, God's victory cannot be glorified without exalting his holy cross. The Holy Cross proclaims the power of the God, a power that turned defeat into triumph through sacrificial love. Even though the cross of Christ reminded the early faithful of the disgrace and humiliation of the Roman form of execution, it clearly recalled for them Christ's resurrection from the dead.

As a sacred symbol of the spiritual life, the Holy Cross has a special place in Orthodox Christian faith and worship. The Holy Cross is so important that two great holy days are observed by the Church to remind the faithful of the beauty of the Holy Cross. The Church from early times specified these two days.

The first of these events is the Exaltation of the Holy Cross on September 14. This great feast celebrates four historical events:

- ✦ Constantine's vision of the cross on October 28, 312, at the Milvian Bridge
- ✦ The finding of the true Cross by St. Helena, Constantine's mother, on her pilgrimage to Jerusalem
- ✦ The consecration of the Church of the Holy Resurrection on September 14, 335
- ✦ The recovery of the true Cross from the Persians in 629

The second holiday dedicated to the Holy Cross occurs on the third Sunday of Lent. This day also recounts the finding of the true Cross by Helena. The Church commemorates this event and refers to this Sunday as the Veneration of the Cross.

In addition to the two feasts honoring the Holy Cross, another day, August 1, was designated to venerate the Holy Cross. This event had its origin in the twelfth century. The day is referred to as the Procession of the Holy Cross. The Greeks, who were under the reign of Emperor Manuel, and the Russians, ruled by Prince Andrew, wanted to commemorate simultaneous victories. The Russians had defeated the Bulgarians, and the Greeks had pushed back the Saracens.

It was decreed that the feast begin on July 31. The true Cross was carried from the imperial court to a church near the Church of Holy Wisdom (Hagia Sophia) in Constantinople. The true Cross was met by a priest, who then led the procession of the true Cross to a baptistery for a blessing of the water. Following the blessing, the true Cross was transferred to the altar of the Hagia Sophia on August 1. After being placed on the altar and remaining there for a brief time, the true Cross was taken on a fourteen-day procession through the streets of Constantinople. The people were able to venerate the true Cross. After fourteen days, the true Cross was returned to the church in the imperial palace.

There was a reason for choosing the first fifteen days of August for this procession. More illnesses occurred during this time than during the rest of the year. The true Cross was carried about the city to sanctify the air, homes, and marketplaces. It also gave good health to all those whom it passed and to those who touched it.

In addition to these three events, the Holy Cross is venerated in the matins service of Holy Friday, when it is brought out from the altar for the faithful to see and venerate it.

The meaning of the cross holds an important place in the everyday life of the Orthodox Christian. Christ gave the faithful these clear instructions: "If anyone desires to come after Me, let him deny himself and take up his cross and follow Me" (Matt 16:24). For the Orthodox Christian, this passage is the center of the faith.

Historically, the cross and the sign of the cross have been important to Christians. But in the early days of Christianity, the cross was not prevalent as a symbol of the faith. It was not wise for the early Christians to announce publicly that they were followers of Christ because they were likely to experience serious persecutions. For safety, they began using signs to identify themselves to one another.

One of the early practices was to make the sign of the cross on one's forehead. The thumb and forefinger were used to make this sign. It is interesting to note that making the sign of the cross did not begin with Christianity. In the Old Testament, there is a reference to a sign or a mark on the forehead (Ezek 9:4–6). (This practice still exists today: some Orthodox priests make the sign of the cross on their foreheads prior to reading the Gospel.) The motion of making the sign of the cross was not noticeable to non-Christians.

Later, the sign of the cross was made by touching the head with the thumb and two fingers, then vertically to the body, up to the left shoulder, and across to the right shoulder, thus drawing a cross on the body. Making of the sign of the cross was not only a signal to other Christians, but it also allowed a Christian in a moment of temptation to step back, "recollect" himself or herself, and find strength in God.

It is not known who first originated the action of making the sign of the cross. It was such a common practice that early scholars did not find it necessary to write about it. However, St. Meletius, Patriarch of Antioch, respected by both the Orthodox and the Arian bishops, was asked to give further proof of the divinity of Jesus. Meletius raised three fingers of the right hand—the thumb, the index and the middle finger—and bent the other two. He said that the three fingers represented the Holy Trinity. He then raised the thumb and the other two fingers to show that they were one and also of the same substance. An Orthodox prayer book compiled by Seraphim Nasser credits Meletius with making the sign of the cross, noting that it was copied from Ignatius Martyr, Patriarch of Antioch.

Furthermore, Hippolytus (ca. 220) wrote that faithful Christians of his time made a habit of making the sign of the cross. From the early days of Christianity, the sign of the cross was used in the Sacraments of Baptism and Confirmation. Eventually, it found its way into the Divine Liturgy.

In the fourth century, St. Basil wrote that the Church teaches in two ways: through writing and through sermons (teachings). He wrote that through teaching we learn to write and make the sign of the cross, which signifies our hope in our Lord Jesus Christ.

The sign of the cross is fundamental and indispensable in the life of the Orthodox Christian. Faithful Orthodox Christians begin the day by making the sign of the cross and saying morning prayers. The day ends with the sign of the cross and the recitation of the evening prayers. The sign of the cross is used at mealtimes; it is used to begin a journey, a chore, or an event; it is used to celebrate happiness and to give comfort in sorrow. Additionally, the sign of the cross is made many times during the Divine Liturgy and other services of the Church.

Making the sign of the cross on one's body is a proclamation that one is a Christian who believes in God as Holy Trinity. The sign of the cross indicates a complete dedication of the self to God. We dedicate our mind so that we can learn and understand the truths of our faith. As we continue the downward stroke of the cross, we dedicate our heart to show that our love for God is first above anything else. And lastly, when we cross our shoulders, we dedicate our strength to work and serve Christ. This dedication is designed to help one fulfill the first and greatest of the commandments: "Thou shall love the Lord thy God with all thy heart, and with all thy soul, and with all thy mind and with all thy strength."

There are many ways of making the sign of the cross. The most common is with the right hand. The thumb, the index finger, and the middle finger are joined together at the tips. This expresses the Holy Trinity. The other two fingers are pressed down to the palm. These two fingers represent the two natures of Christ and that God the Son became Man and came down to earth to save us.

The sign of the cross is made by touching the forehead, the heart, then the right shoulder and finally the left shoulder. During this movement, this prayer is said: "Holy God, Holy Mighty, Holy Immortal, have mercy on us." Another prayer to recite, "In the name of the Father, Son, and Holy Spirit." Traditionally, the sign of the cross is made three times.

The sign of the cross is more than an action. It is a statement of faith in the Father, Son, and Holy Spirit, and ends with "amen." The word *amen* means "yes, it is true." Andreopoulos writes that amen "expresses a joy and triumphant expression of God." The complete sign of the cross professes that all three human faculties—the mental, emotional, and spiritual—together with one's tenacity, are dedicated to the service of God. St. Cyril of Jerusalem wrote:

> Let us not be ashamed to confess the Crucified. Be the
> Cross our seal, made with boldness of our fingers . . .
> over the bread we eat and the cup we drink . . . before
> we sleep, when we lie down and when we wake; when
> we are traveling and when we are at rest.

The Orthodox Christian has an extraordinary devotion to and deep faith in the cross of Christ. This sacred and esteemed cross, as a symbol of spiritual life, is foremost in the life of the Orthodox Christian. This Holy Cross, a symbol of victory over death, is worn by the faithful from the day of baptism in Christ to the falling asleep in the Lord. Christ said to His disciples, "Follow Me," and the Orthodox Christian follows Christ dutifully in His service and sacrifice.

O Lord, save Thy people and bless thine inheritance.
Grant victories for the Orthodox Christians over their adversaries,
And by the virtue of Thy Cross preserve Thy habitation.

Troparia: Exaltation of the Holy Cross*

* *Tchaikovsky incorporated this hymn, with the music of the Russian Church, into his "Overture of 1812."*

Chapter 6

CROSSES IN ANTIQUITY

Ankh Cross

We receive the cross when we are baptized in Christ's name. It is a privilege to wear the Christian cross, so we should do it respectfully and reverently. The symbol of our faith is hung around our neck, it is embossed on rings for our fingers, and it hangs from the walls of our churches and in the rooms of our homes. We even hang the cross from the mirrors of our automobiles. Some Ethiopian Orthodox Christians, especially women, tattoo the symbol of the cross on their bodies. Moreover, we build churches in the shape of a cross. The cross adorns the flags of several nations. And above all, we make the sign of the cross on our bodies, which enables us to physically and visually fulfill St. Paul's admonition, "Glory is in the cross." But where and when did the symbol of the cross originate?

The originator of the design of the cross is unknown. The question about the invention of the cross lies in the realm of "Who invented fire?" or "Who made the first pottery?" The sheer plainness of the cross, its simplicity, allowed it to be used as a religious symbol, as an ornament and as a means of execution of humans from the beginning of civilization.

It is known that ancient peoples worshipped many gods and often used the cross as a religious figure in worshipping their gods. The cross symbol has existed through all of ancient history, and it appeared in many shapes and forms. Actually though, for every clan, tribe, or culture, the cross symbol with its various shapes and forms had different meanings.

In some early cultures, the two arms of a cross were symbolic of life and living. In various clans or tribes, the horizontal arms of the cross referred to the earth and its people. However, only the members of the clan or tribe knew the meaning of their cross symbol.

The symbol of the cross, a design of two intersecting lines, is a very simple, ancient design. Many, many centuries before the rise of Christianity, early humans used the symbol. Prehistoric humans etched the symbol in their caves. The cross symbol is found on ancient objects they made. Ancient peoples liked finery and used the cross symbol in jewelry. In fact, some wore the cross on a piece of leather around the neck.

The cross design has been found not only in pottery and jewelry, but also in ancient weavings, carvings, and paintings. Vases and urns with variations of the cross design have been found in all ancient cultures. Ancient man had obviously begun to beautify his surroundings.

Early peoples not only beautified their environment but also had another use for the cross. In ancient times, a human effigy was hung on a cross. We know that ancient human beings were very superstitious and had many gods to worship. Mere existence depended on the whims of nature. Proper climatic conditions were important for survival. In his pleas to his many gods for good weather and crops, the sacrificed human would be removed from the cross and chopped into pieces. Portions of blood and flesh were then distributed to the members of the clan to be buried. This was done to petition the gods for a good crop.

The cross symbol was used by ancients on every continent of the earth. For instance, the North American Indians used the cross design, as did the Aztecs of Mesoamerica. In Europe, among the Nordic peoples and others, the cross symbol was part of daily life. Even in Asia and the Middle East, the cross was found. Surprisingly, the cross symbol was also found with the people of the Pacific islands.

Archaeologists agree that the earliest people to use the symbol of the cross were probably from the steppes of Asia. From the simple

design of two intersecting lines, the swastika was developed. It is believed that the swastika is of Sanskrit origin. For the Aryans, who worshipped fire, the arms of the swastika represented the two sticks rubbed together to make a fire.

The swastika cross took on many forms. In some instances, the arms turn from left to right instead of right to left. The meaning for this symbol is "good omen" or "good fortune." It has been found on the pottery and jewelry of most of the early civilizations. Unfortunately, the swastika has suffered from its infamous use by the Nazis in Germany before and during World War II.

Another example of the oldest and most universal cross is the solar cross. It has several names, including the sun, sun wheel, sun disc,

and Odin's cross. The ancient people of northern Europe worshipped the god Odin, whose emblem was a cross enclosed in a circle.

The solar cross was in common use. It has been found chiseled in stone in Paleolithic caves of the Pyrenees, in megalithic sites in Scotland, in Mesopotamia, and on the Iranian plateau, as well as in the cities of the Indus River valley. This cross symbol was used everywhere.

The solar cross was not the only cross used by ancient humans. Another shape of cross appeared throughout the ancient world. This new form was in the shape of the letter T, and it is known as the tau (Greek for T) cross. Some historians believe that a two-beamed cross had its origin in ancient Chaldea, a region of Mesopotamia situated between the Euphrates River and the Persian Gulf.

In Sumerian, Babylonian, and Assyrian mythology, Tammuz was the god of animal and plant fertility. Tammuz corresponded with the Phoenician god known to the Greeks as Adonis. Since T was the first letter of Tammuz, the T or tau cross was used as his symbol. When the worshippers of Tammuz were initiated into the mysteries of the cult, they were marked with a T on their foreheads.

The Phoenicians also knew the tau cross, since it was the emblem of their goddess Astarte. They used the tau cross as a seal to mark and identify their properties.

It is thought by some that the tau cross symbol appeared in Egypt around 3030 BC. For the people of ancient Egypt, the tau cross was the symbol of the god Osiris, and it represented "breath of life." Osiris was the god of fertility and eternal life after death. His wife and sister, Isis, personified the virtues of the wife and mother. Her emblem was an oval.

The tau cross of the god Osiris and the oval of the goddess were combined: the oval placed on top of the tau became the ankh cross. This emblem is on many Egyptian statues and in hieroglyphics. Interestingly, the early Christian Church in Alexandria, Egypt, adopted the ankh cross as a Christian symbol.

Another cross in the culture of Babylon (modern day Iraq) appeared on the scene in history. It was the emblem for their sun god, Baal. The symbol for Baal was a cross within a double circle. Baal was the ancient Semitic god and was worshipped by the Canaanites and the Phoenicians. Even so, the Hebrews considered Baal a false god.

The tau cross is called the "cross of the Old Testament." Some historians say that the Israelites may have been familiar with this cross because they were in Egyptian bondage for 120 years and may have used it. One incident cited to show the possible use of the cross by the Israelites is found in the celebration of Passover, as described in Exodus 12, and the deliverance of the Israelites from Egypt. A male lamb was slain and a stain of the lamb's blood was made on the side posts and lintels of their houses. This was done so God would "pass over" them when the firstborn sons of the Egyptians were slain. However, after checking with rabbis, it was learned that the tau cross was not used. Instead, a dab of the lamb's blood was used to mark the doors.

Another instance of the Israelites possibly using the symbol of the cross is found in the Book of Esther. The story tells of the hanging of Haman on the gallows. The story took place in Persia, where Esther was the queen of Emperor Xerxes. Haman was seeking revenge on Mordecai, a Jew who was Esther's uncle. Haman plotted the execution of Mordecai and the extermination of all the Jews in the empire. Queen Esther discovered the plot and reported it to Xerxes, who was unaware that she was Jewish. This revelation could have meant her life, but Xerxes was tolerant and he confronted Haman. The instigator, Haman, was found guilty and hanged on the gallows he had constructed for Mordecai. Again, after checking with a rabbi, it was learned that the definition of "gallows" is obscure and "being hung" does not indicate that the gallows were in the shape of a cross.

Apparently, ancient writers attempted to show that the cross symbol was also used by the Israelites. The theme of this book is the cross, not "might have beens." Discussion of these incidents must be left to theologians and biblical historians.

Continuing in the search of the use of the cross in ancient cultures, we find that the cross symbol was used in ancient Greece. The Greek  cross, a symbol of four equal arms, was well known and used in Minoan Crete as a symbol of worship. To the ancient Greeks this equilateral cross signified the four corners of the earth—north, south, east, and west—or the four winds. Furthermore, it symbolized the four indestructible elements: earth, water, fire, and air.

Not only did the Greeks use the cross symbol for worship, but they also used it as a decorative design on pottery, vases, and urns. Ancient artifacts show ladies wearing gold and silver crosses in their ears and around their necks.

The Romans also used the tau cross. Unlike the Phoenicians and the Egyptians, the Romans called the tau cross the "sign of life." For the Romans this was a symbol of great divinity. The official garments of the pagan priests were marked with the tau cross. Even the Roman rulers held it in their hands to show their authority was divinely given.

Amazingly, the Romans used the tau cross as a religious symbol. The temple of the goddess Vesta was in the Roman forum, which was attended to by six virgin priestesses. These Vestal Virgins were given special privileges. As a decorative ornament, they wore the tau cross around their necks.

Not only was the cross used in the pleasantries of daily life of the ancient Romans, but it was also an instrument of executions. History has led us to believe that only the Romans used the cross as a means of capital punishment. This is not true. Execution by crucifixion was used by all cultures. The execution on the cross was a punishment inflicted on hardened criminals, atrocious murderers, enemies, and slaves. Some victims were spiked to the earth with a cross driven through their bodies. The unburied bodies were left to rot or to be eaten by birds and beasts.

The ancient Greeks had various forms of execution. The most common form of execution was for the criminal to drink poison. Execution by the cross was rarely used, but it was used as an instrument of execution for certain crimes. It is recorded that Alexander the Great used the cross to execute 2,000 Tyrians.

In ancient Rome, the methods of execution were selected so that the amount of suffering was equivalent to the seriousness of the crime. The class or status of the criminal was also taken into consideration. A Roman citizen might be given the option to commit suicide, while a lower class citizen had no options. He was crucified.

The Romans used crucifixion as a means of keeping the conquered people afraid of Roman power. An example of this occurred in 4 BC, when Herod the Great, King of Judea, died. There were many pretenders to his position. In addition, there were those who wanted to use his death as an opening to rebel against Rome. The rebels struck and took control of the city of Jerusalem. The Romans could not allow this. They called for help and Roman armies from the area descended on the towns and villages. The strength of the Roman armies quelled every rebellion.

To demonstrate to what lengths the Romans would go to maintain control of Jerusalem, they killed more than 2,000 Jews by execution. The 2,000 crosses were erected close together, and on each cross hung a Jewish rebel. The victims were left to die and were not buried. Instead they were left to be eaten by wild birds.

In Judea, the Romans generally observed the Mosaic law when they crucified Hebrew convicts. In Deuteronomy 21:23, we read, "His body shall not remain overnight on the tree, but you shall surely bury him that day, so that you do not defile the land which the Lord your God is giving you as an inheritance; for he who is hanged is accursed of God." Therefore, the bodies of Hebrew convicts in Judea were removed and buried before nightfall except in certain cases, such as the incident of King Herod crucifying 2,000 Jews.

There is hardly an ancient culture where the cross has not been found. Even the ancient Celts worshipped the cross symbol centuries before the birth of Christ. The word "Celt" comes from the ancient Greek word *keltoi*, meaning "barbarian." They were so named by the ancient Greek historian Herodotus.

About 300 BC, the Celts, a large cohesive tribe, began to break up. Many tribes began wandering in search of new lands. In the fourth century, the Celts invaded the Greco-Roman world. They did not come quietly, for in 390 BC, they plundered Rome. A century later, in 297 BC, they sacked Delphi in Greece.

The Celts traveled far into Asia Minor. They remained in that region and became known as the Galatians. The Romans referred to the Continental European Celts as the *Galli*, or Gauls. The Celts in the British Isles were named the *Britianni*. One story tells that when the Celts, who were blond, blue-eyed, and fair-skinned, invaded the

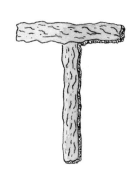

Mediterranean lands, the local people with dark hair, eyes, and olive complexions were astonished. They referred to the people as *galla*, the Greek work for "milk"—thus the name "Galatians."

In their religion the Celts had priests called druids. The ancient druids worshipped the sun and took as a symbol of their god a living tree. In celebrating their devotion to the sun, the druids assembled in small woodlands to select a majestic oak tree. This was a symbol of their deity. The druids then cut the branches off the sides of the tree and fastened the two largest branches to the highest part of the trunk. The trunk of the tree, with the attached branches, resembled a huge cross. In several places on the bark, they carved a symbol of one of their gods.

In their wanderings, the Celts saw different designs on the pottery, urns, vases, and jewelry used by the people in the territories they invaded and settled. They liked what they saw and incorporated many designs into their own works. For instance, the Celts adopted plant motifs from Greece and elliptical curves, spirals, and chevrons from the people of the steppes. These designs appeared on painted pottery, shields, swords, helmets, bowls, and jewelry.

One of their designs was a cross symbol. The Celts added a circle to the cross, which is now known as the Celtic cross. This cross also predates Christianity. For the Celts, this cross symbol was associated with fertility. The cross represented the male generative power, and the circle indicated the female.

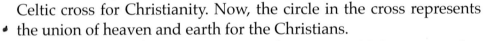

In the fifth century St. Patrick went to Ireland to Christianize the Celts. There, he found Celtic crosses, mainly made of stone. He adopted the Celtic cross for Christianity. Now, the circle in the cross represents the union of heaven and earth for the Christians.

Not only was the cross known in the Old World, but it was also known in the New World. When Cortez arrived in Mexico in 1521, he saw that the Aztecs had the cross symbol. One of his lieutenants found many large stone crosses during his explorations from the island of Cozumel to the Yucatán Peninsula. The Spaniards were so astonished to find these crosses that they immediately consecrated them as objects of worship.

The cross symbol has existed through all ages in some shape or form. Furthermore, it has differed among various ancient civilizations. It is the oldest universal symbol. Ancient peoples used it in their everyday lives, but the cross symbol did not have universal meaning. The symbol meant different things to different people. The horizontal arms could represent one thing to one tribe and yet have a completely different meaning for another clan. The same was true of the vertical arms. The most common understanding was that they represented the four points of the compass. Another common meaning among the ancient people was the representation of earth, fire, water, and air. The ancient cross had a religious purpose and was connected with some form of nature worship. All in all, the symbol of the cross had a significant and vital influence among the ancient peoples.

Crosses are ladders that lead to heaven.

St. Ephraim of Syria

Chapter 7

CROSSES IN OTHER CULTURES

Chinese Cross

Amazingly, the symbol of the cross is not only associated with ancient civilizations, but it is also found in many modern cultures. For example, the cross appears in Chinese culture. The Chinese have a saying that God fashioned the earth in the shape of the cross. Their symbol is an equilateral cross in a square. For them, the four ends of the cross represent the four points of the compass: north, south, east, and west.

Likewise, Native Americans have the cross symbol in their cultures. Although the North American Indians are made up of many nations and languages, their religions have a main goal: to improve their relationship with Mother Nature and her creatures and to live in harmony with the universe. Since there are many tribes, various signs and symbols are in use.

One ceremony that is common among the Native American nations is the ceremony of the sweat lodge. There are variations in the ceremony among tribes, but they are not of major significance. For this ritual, an outdoor area is marked with a large circle and four willow poles are buried, the thick end down, in the outline of the circle. The narrow ends of the poles are tied together to form a point. These four poles form a cross. In addition, a colored flag is attached to each pole. The colors of the flags are red, black, gold, and green, symbolizing north, south, east, and west. A fire is built in the structure for the ritual ceremony. After the ceremony, the participants experience an exhilarating feeling of being reborn.

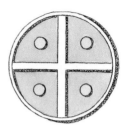

Various North American tribes use crosses with special meanings known only to the members of that tribe. For example, the Hopi Indians in Arizona use a cross inscribed in a circle with a small circle in each quadrant of the cross. The circle represents the world and corresponds to the outermost visible horizon. There, the sun passes on its way through the year. The points of the cross represent the solstices and the equinoxes. Also, the points refer to the four directions. The four circles symbolize the four nations (there are many tribes in each nation) that keep the world in balance.

Similarly, in Hinduism there is also an equilateral cross symbol. The vertical arm represents the higher states of being, while the horizontal arm refers to the earthly states. In addition, the swastika cross is in the Buddhist religion. For the followers of Buddhism, the swastika is a symbol for the Buddha's mind. It is also a symbol of virtue and goodwill.

In summary, every culture has the cross symbol. Yet the interpretation varies by culture. The meaning is not universal. For some the emblem represents the four points of the compass. For others, the cross has philosophical and spiritual significance. For yet other cultures, the cross symbol defines the solstices and the equinoxes of the year. Each culture used the cross symbol, but it was not generally as important of an aspect of society as it has been in Christianity.

For as I was passing through and considering the objects of your worship, I even found an altar with this inscription:
TO THE UNKNOWN GOD
Therefore, the One whom you worship without knowing, Him I proclaim to you. . . .

Acts 17:23

Chapter 8

The Holy Crosses

The Orthodox Church does not use symbols for symbols' sake. There is a real purpose for the symbols: to convey an idea or thought to the faithful. Just as icons transmit the stories to the people, the cross of Christ conveys the ultimate power of God to the faithful.

From the three simplest cross shapes—the tau cross, the Greek cross, and the Latin cross—there are now more than 400 types of Christian crosses incorporating these shapes. Many new crosses were derived during the age of heraldry. The Crusades led to the beginning of heraldry. Many Christian crosses were designed to identify each group who was participating in the battles. But there are also many ancient Christian crosses. Every cross has a teaching. Behind it is a story that tells of an event that led to the creation of that cross.

ALPHA AND OMEGA CROSS   This cross is a tau cross with the first and last letters of the Greek alphabet attached to the crossbar. This early cross symbolizes "God who is" the beginning and the end (Rev 22:13).

ALPHA AND OMEGA ON THE CHI-RHO CROSS   This fifth-century chi-rho cross includes the Greek letters A (*alpha*) and Ω (*omega*). Again, this symbolizes "God who is" the beginning and the end (Rev 22:13).

ANKH CROSS   This symbol originated in ancient Egyptian culture. In the early days of Christianity, the Coptic Christian churches in Egypt adopted the ankh cross as a Christian symbol. This cross is also known as the "key of the Nile," looped tau cross, or the Ansate cross. (*Ansate* means "with a handle" or "shaped like a handle.")

ANCHOR CROSS   The Christians adopted the ship's anchor as a symbol because the anchor is in the shape of the cross. The early Christians adopted it as their symbol for hope and dedication. They took the symbolic meaning from Hebrews 6:19: "This hope we have as an anchor of the soul, both sure and steadfast, and which enters the Presence behind the veil." ("Behind the veil" is a reference to heaven.)

ANCHOR CROSS WITH ICTHYS This symbol was found in the catacombs. It had the anchor with either a fish suspended from the crossbar or the Greek letters A (*alpha*) and Ω (*omega*). The fish represented the Greek word for fish, ΙΧΘΥΣ (*icthys*), a code word for *Jesus Christ Soter*, Jesus Christ the Savior.

CELTIC CROSS The Celtic cross combines cross and circle. In the fifth century, St. Patrick found the Celtic cross in Ireland. He adopted it as a Christian cross. The circle around the arms of the cross represents the sun and eternity. The circle, a symbol of Irish Christianity, represents the union of heaven and earth.

CHI-RHO CROSS The Greek letters Χ (*chi*) and Γ (*rho*) are the first letters in the word *Christos*. The chi-rho cross is a monogram of the name Jesus Christ. St. Constantine the Great, before the battle at Milvian Bridge, saw the chi-rho cross in the sky with the words εν τούτο νίκα (*en touto nika*, "in this sign conquer"). He had his soldiers mark their shields with the symbol, and they were victorious. This led to Constantine's conversion to Christianity. The cross is also known as the Labarum.

COPTIC CROSS This ancient Coptic cross is comprised of four equal arms that each end in three points. The points represent the Holy Trinity—Father, Son, and Holy Spirit. The three points on each arm total twelve points, and these represent the Holy Apostles.

EASTERN ORTHODOX, RUSSIAN, OR SLAVIC CROSS   The three-bar cross is of Greek origin. At the beginning of the ninth century, crucifixes began to be seen with the lower bar on the cross. This lower bar provided a place for Christ to rest his feet. Between the tenth and eleventh centuries, the Slavonic churches began placing the lower bar at an angle.

A second cross is inscribed in the trefoil cross. Its foot board is slanted from left to right. The trefoil cross symbolizes the Holy Trinity, for the three-fold cluster is joined as one.

There are several explanations for the slanted foot bar of the cross-within-a-cross:

1. The slanted foot bar serves as a reprimand to those who believe that Christ did not actually suffer on the cross, but only seemed to suffer. The inclined bar shows the agony was so great that His nailed feet strained loose the nailed part of the cross when He pushed on the board.

2. Another interpretation is that the right side of the tilted board shows the lightened burden of believers and the left side indicated the weighing down of the nonbelievers.

3. Lastly, the slanted board symbolizes the part played by the two thieves who were crucified with Christ. The thief on the right is on the raised end of the board, and the lowered left side represents the thief who cursed Christ.

The small crossbar at the top of the cross represents the inscription "This is Jesus, King of the Jews" written in Greek, Latin, and Hebrew.

FOS-ZOE CROSS   This cross is known as the light and life cross. It appeared around the eighth century. It is a Greek cross with the vertical letters ΦΩΣ (*fos*, Greek for "light") and the horizontal letters ZWH (*zoe*, "life"). This is a symbol of regeneration as a result of partaking Holy Communion. The zoe cross also refers to Christ, who is our Light and Life.

GOLGOTHA CROSS   The Golgotha cross is composed of a large Latin cross with two small crosses in the lower quadrants. The large cross represents the cross on which Jesus was crucified. The small crosses are for the two thieves who were crucified with Christ.

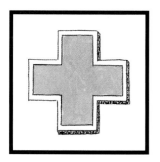

GREEK CROSS   The Greek cross was one of the early crosses from antiquity, and it has four arms of equal length. The Greek cross was adopted as a Christian symbol. The Red Cross Association adopted the Greek cross as its symbol.

JERUSALEM CROSS   The Jerusalem cross contains thirteen crosses. It has eight tau crosses, a cross in each quadrant, and the cross itself. The entire cross represents Christ and his Twelve Apostles. The small crosses represent the four Evangelists: Mark, Matthew, Luke, and John. Some report that the four crosses represent the four directions in which the word of Christ spread from Jerusalem. This cross is not to be confused with the Crusaders' cross, which is not constructed with the tau cross.

LATIN CROSS   The Latin cross is a common cross in Christianity. The horizontal piece is shorter than the vertical piece. The cross represents the redeeming martyrdom of Jesus when he was crucified on the True Cross.

MALTA CROSS   The origin of this cross is unknown. It is the oldest cross in heraldry. Some believe that it has an Arabic motif. It can also be considered a geometric design, as seen on ancient mosques in Jerusalem, Damascus, and Baghdad, and also found in Europe and in Sicily. By the thirteenth century, the cross of Malta was a common heraldic symbol in England, France, Germany, and Poland.

The four arms represent the cross of Jesus, and the eight points symbolize the Beatitudes that He taught during the Sermon on the Mount (Matt 5:3–10):

1. Blessed are the poor in spirit, for theirs is the kingdom of heaven.

2. Blessed are they that mourn, for they shall be comforted.

3. Blessed are the meek, for they shall inherit the earth.

4. Blessed are those who hunger and thirst for righteousness, for they shall be filled.

5. Blessed are the merciful, for they shall obtain mercy.

6. Blessed are the pure in heart, for they shall see God.

7. Blessed are the peacemakers, for they shall be called the children of God.

8. Blessed are those who are persecuted for righteousness' sake, for theirs is the kingdom of heaven.

THE PAPAL CROSS The official emblem of the Roman Catholic papal office is used by the Pope. The papal cross's three crossbars represent the Pope's realms of religious authority—the Church, the world, and heaven.

PASSION CROSS (CALVARY CROSS) Erected on a base of three steps, this cross symbolizes the Holy Trinity. The steps also represent the three Christian virtues: faith, hope, and charity. The four points of the cross are a reminder that the redeemed were from the four quarters of the earth.

PECTORAL CROSS This is the earliest known cross worn by a bishop. It dates back to 461 AD, when Pope Hilarius wore a cross over the breast. The pectoral cross is part of a bishop's attire. The cross is worn outside the robes and is a reminder that the bishop should not merely carry Christ in his heart, but must confess Him in the face of all men as he preaches the faith of Christ.

The pectoral cross is a bejeweled cross made of fine metal. It is suspended by a chain over the breast of the bishop, and has a relic encased in the cross.

PILGRIM CROSS Pilgrims on their way to Jerusalem to visit the Holy Land and to pray at the tomb of Christ had the custom of carrying a small metal cross with them. The long vertical arm was sharpened at the bottom so that the cross could be driven into the ground. The pilgrim would stick the cross into the ground as protection while he or she slept and rested on the long, tiresome journey.

ST. ANDREW'S CROSS St. Andrew was the first (*protokletos* in Greek) of the apostles to be called by Jesus. Andrew suffered martyrdom in the town of Patras, Greece. At Patras, Andrew cured and converted Maximilla, wife of the pagan proconsul, Aegeates. Andrew also converted Maximilla's brother, Stratocles. After hearing the Gospel from Andrew, Maximilla denied Aegeates his marital rights because he was a pagan. Aegeates had Andrew thrown into prison. There he was beaten and then condemned to be crucified.

Stratocles wanted to rescue Andrew, but the apostle refused and was tied to a cross. Andrew remained alive for two days continually preaching to his people. Stratocles and Maximilla buried his body.

Subsequently, Andrew's coffin was taken to Constantinople in AD 337. When Constantinople fell in the Fourth Crusade in 1204, Andrew's skull was taken to Amalfi, Italy, and the face bones were taken to St. Peter's in Rome. In September 1965, Pope Paul VI returned the relics in a reliquary to Athenagoras, the Ecumenical Patriarch, who then returned the reliquary to Patras, Greece.

The reliquary is enshrined at the church of St. Andrew.

Tradition has it that Andrew was crucified on an X-shaped cross. Some historians write that most likely his cross was a tau cross, but by the Middle Ages, it became an X cross—the X representing *chi* for *Christos*.

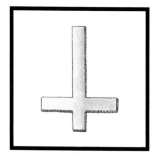

ST. PETER'S CROSS   This is an inverted cross. When St. Peter was to be executed on an upright cross, he said that he was not worthy to be crucified in the same way as his Lord. He was therefore crucified upside down. The inverted cross represents humility.

TAU CROSS   The tau cross is a cross taken from antiquity. It is the shape of the letter T and was adopted by the early Christians as a Christian symbol.

TREFOIL CROSS   The trefoil cross is a cross with the arms ending in a threefold cluster. The three-fold clusters signify the Trinity.

IC XC NIKA This cross with the sacred monogram of IC XC is one of the most ancient of the sacred monograms of Christianity. This cross has the Greek letters arranged between the arms. The letters IC are the first and last letters of the Greek word Ιεσους (*Jesus*), and XC are the first and last letters of Χριστος (*Christos*), as they appear in Byzantine script. The bottom letters, NIKA, are a single word that means "conquers." Together the words read, "Jesus Christ conquers."

The word of the cross is called the power of God,
because the might of God, that is, His victory over death,
has been revealed through it.

St. John of Damascus

The information about the crosses is from the following references:

Miranda Bruce-Mitford, *Illustrated Book of Signs and Symbols* (DK, 1996).

George Ferguson, *Signs and Symbols in Christian Art* (Oxford University Press, 1966).

David Fontana, *The Secret Language of Symbols* (Chronicle Books, 1994).

J. C. J. Metford, *Dictionary of Christian Lore and Legend* (Thames & Husdon, 1991).

David Talbot Rice, *Art of the Byzantine Era* (Thames & Husdon, 1985).

Johannes Troyer, *The Cross as Symbol and Ornament* (Philadelphia: Westminster Press, 1961).

EPILOGUE

The cross symbol has been with human civilization since antiquity. For the ancient peoples, the cross served as an element of their religions, a component of ambience, an adornment of attire, and an instrument of execution. The cross symbol was not revered, and it meant different things to different people.

Approximately 2,000 years ago, a simple wooden cross was erected at Calvary, outside the walls of Jerusalem. It was looked upon as a symbol of disgrace, but later it assumed a different meaning, a meaning that encompassed the world. The Holy Cross is recognized universally as a symbol of Christianity, and it has an esteemed place in the Christian faith. Today, no symbol or emblem has more worldwide significance than the cross of Jesus Christ.

Christ's crucifixion on the cross gave new meaning to the simple shape. His crucifixion converted the cross from a symbol of shame and humility into a symbol of salvation. The message the Holy Cross brings is salvation by faith, service, and sacrifice. The early Christians suffered persecutions and ridicule, yet they had faith and many were sacrificed. There were those brave Christians who preached the word of Christ in dangerous environments, yet they had faith, and they served and were martyred. St. Paul taught about Christ. He preached, "But God forbid that I should glory, save in the cross of our Lord Jesus Christ, by whom the world is crucified unto me, and I unto the world" (Gal 6:14). St. Paul served and he was sacrificed.

Through the centuries Christians have fought to save and glorify the cross. Constantine the Great gave the cross honor. His aging mother, St. Helena, traveled to Jerusalem and located the True Cross for all humanity to see and adore. Heraklios fought battles to recover the True Cross from the Muslims. Untold saints and martyrs have died for the cross.

For these people, the cross was not just a symbol of their faith. It was an object of their devotion. They sacrificed their lives for the cross. Terrible deeds have been done in His name—tortures, persecutions, inquisitions, crusades, theological disagreements, religious wars—all in the name of Jesus. Through all, Christianity and the cross have prevailed.

The Holy Cross for the Orthodox Christian is a symbol of supreme sacrifice and resurrection. The Holy Cross continues to be a personal protection against the evils of the world. The greatest historical wrong was the crucifixion of Christ. His crucifixion pardoned our sins, and His resurrection assures us victory over death. For these reasons Orthodox Christians adore and venerate the cross.

Eighteen centuries ago, on September 14, 335, the bishop of Jerusalem, Makarios, took the True Cross outside the Church of the Holy Resurrection. (The True Cross had recently been found by St. Helena.) He stood on a large pulpit, the ambo, and held the True Cross high for the faithful people to see it. Those faithful worshippers were so awed and elated to see the True Cross that they cried out *Kyrie, Eleison* ("Lord, have mercy"). This simple symbol—the

True Cross—excited the pious people so much that they shouted their passion for their faith. Today, we stand in awe and ponder its influence in today's world.

The power of the cross of Christ has filled the world.

Athanasius of Alexandria

I am the Alpha and Omega, the Beginning and the End.

Revelation 1:8

GLOSSARY

A

Abraham

The first Patriarch of the Bible was Abraham. He was asked by God to sacrifice his son, Isaac, and was ready to obey God. He was rewarded for obeying God. The Jewish people honor him as the father of the Hebrews through his son Isaac. The Muslims accept Abraham as the father of the Arab people through his son, Ishmael.

Aelia Capitolina

When Herod rebuilt Jerusalem, he gave it the Latin name of Aelia Capitolina.

Alaric the Goth

The Goths were a Germanic barbarian tribe, and Alaric the Goth was their chief. They invaded and devastated Europe between the third and fourth centuries. Alaric invaded Italy, and Rome fell to the Goths in 410 AD.

Alexander the Great

King of Macedonia, Alexander the Great (356–323 BC) conquered most of the ancient world. His conquest extended from Asia Minor to Egypt and India.

Alexandria, Egypt	Alexandria, the city and Mediterranean seaport, is in northern Egypt. Alexander the Great founded it in 322 BC. Alexandria was a major cultural center of the ancient world, and it was renowned for its library and lighthouse.
Ambo	A large pulpit or stand in the early Christian churches is called the ambo. The lesson or other parts of the services were read from the ambo.
Anatolia	The part of modern-day Turkey that forms the westernmost peninsula of Asia is Anatolia.
Apse	The apse is the semicircular part of the church, which is in the east end of the church. The altar is in the apse.
Arab	An Arab is a member of a Semitic Arabic-speaking people who live throughout North Africa and the Middle East.
Arian Controversy	Arius (250–336) led this controversy. He was a priest of the Church of Alexandria. In 318, he began to circulate a Unitarian doctrine that there was only one person in Christ. Arius professed that Father and Son were distinct beings, that the Son had a state of existence before His appearance on Earth. Furthermore, they believed that the messiah was not a real man, but a divine being in the veil of flesh. The Council of Nicaea condemned the heresy in 325. It upheld the Orthodox view of Athanasius, who taught that the Son was "of the same substance with the Father."
Armenia	Armenia, a country in southwestern Asia between the Black and Caspian Seas, is

surrounded by Iran, Turkey, Georgia, and Azerbaijan. Armenia is an ancient country and was one of the first countries to become Christianized.

Aryans

Aryans are, hypothetically, an ethnic group descended from early Indo-Europeans.

Assyria

The ancient Mesopotamian kingdom of Assyria, whose empire extended southwest and eastward, was a great kingdom from the ninth to seventh centuries BC.

Avars

A Caucasian nomadic tribe, the Avars settled in the Roman province in the latter half of the sixth century. They settled in the lands between the Carpathian Mountains and the Danube River.

B

Baal

Baal is the ancient Semitic God of fertility or any of the nature gods worshipped by the Canaanites and the Phoenicians. The ancient Hebrews considered Baal a false god.

Babylon

Babylon, the capital of ancient Babylonia, was an empire in Mesopotamia (modern Iraq). It flourished from the first half of the second millennium until it was conquered by Persia in 539 BC. The city was situated on the Euphrates River. It was noted for its extreme wealth. The Hanging Gardens, located here, were one of the Seven Wonders of the World.

Balkans

The Balkan Mountains are an extension of the Alp Mountains, which run across central Europe. The Balkan Peninsula is in southeastern Europe between the Adriatic and Ionian Seas on the west, and the Aegean and Black Seas in the east. The Sava and the Danube Rivers are considered the northern boundary.

Battle of Salamis	Salamis is an island in eastern Greece near the port of Piraeus. It was the location of a major battle in 480 BC in which the Greeks defeated the Persians.
Bosphorus	The Bosphorus is a strait linking the Black Sea and the Sea of Miramar, separating European and Asian Turkey.
Buddhism	Buddhism is a world religion or philosophy based on the teachings of Buddha. It maintains that by suppressing worldly desires, one can attain a state of enlightenment.
Byzantine Empire	The Byzantine Empire is also referred to as the Eastern or Greek Empire. The Byzantine Empire lasted from the separation of the eastern and western Roman Empire on the death of Theodosius in 395 until the capture of Constantinople by the Turks in 1453. It was the center of Orthodox Christianity.

C

Caesarea	Caesarea was an ancient seaport on the coast of Samaria. It was the Roman capital of Palestine. Modern-day Caesarea is approximately twenty-five miles south of Haifa, Israel.
Canaanite	The Canaanites were members of an ancient Semitic people. They lived in Canaan from 3000 BC until the time of the Israelite conquest around 100 BC.
Catacomb	An underground cemetery in Rome, the catacombs consist of passages or tunnels with

rooms and niches leading off the main tunnels for burial chambers.

Celts	The Celts were ancient Indo-European people. In pre-Roman times, they lived in central and western Europe. They were driven to the western part of the European continent by the Romans and certain Germanic tribes, mostly the Anglos and the Saxons.
Chalcedon	An ancient Greek city, Chalcedon was located on the Bosphorus, near modern Istanbul. This city was founded in 685 BC.
Chaldea	Chaldea was an ancient region of Mesopotamia that was situated between the Euphrates River and the Persian Gulf.
Chosroes	Chosroes was the Great King of Persia who occupied the throne in 531. He was the king of the Sassanians Dynasty. His wars with the Byzantine Empire (part of the Roman Empire) were not to conquer but instead to plunder. He and his armies plundered Antioch in 590.
Chrysopolis	Chrysopolis (formerly Scutari; present-day Üsküdar, Turkey) was a city on the Black Sea. Constantine the Great defeated Licinius in a battle that gave Constantine sole leadership of the Roman Empire.
Constantine the Great	The Roman emperor Constantine converted to Christianity in 312 and also made Christianity a state religion. He moved the capital from Rome to the city of Byzantium, which he then renamed Constantinople in 330.
Constantinople	Constantinople was inaugurated as the capital of the Roman Empire by Constantine in 330. It is now known as Istanbul.

Copt	The name "Copt" was given to the Christians of Egypt. The name is a contraction of the Greek word *aegyptoi* and the Arabic *qibt*, both meaning "Egyptian."
Cozumel	Cozumel is an island not far from Cancun, Mexico.
Crusades	The Crusades were any of several religious expeditions by Western European Christians in the eleventh and thirteenth centuries to retake area captured by Muslim forces.
Ctesiphon	Ctesiphon was the capital city of the Persians during the Sassanian dynasty. It is now modern-day Baghdad.
Caucasus	The Caucasus mountain range forms the boundary between Europe and Asia.

D

Damascus	One of the oldest cities in the world is Damascus. It is believed to be inhabited since 2000 BC. Damascus is the capital of modern-day Syria.
Danube River	The Danube River is the longest river in Western Europe. It rises in the Black Forest of western Germany and empties into the Black Sea.
Delphi	Delphi is an ancient Greek town on the southern slopes of Mount Parnassus. It is the site of the Temple of Apollo and the Delphic Oracle. The Celts plundered Delphi in 297 BC.
Diocletian	Diocletian was proclaimed the emperor of Rome in 284. He attempted to restore the pagan religion by persecuting Christians. He failed and abdicated in 305.

Diptych	A diptych is a pair of icons hinged to form two panels.
Druids	Druids were priests of an ancient religion practiced in Britain, Ireland, and Gaul until the people of those areas were converted to Christianity.

E

Edict of Milan	The Edict of Milan was proclaimed by Constantine and Licinius after the conquest of Italy in 312. This edict secured for the Christians the restitution of their civil and religious rights.
Egeria	Egeria was a Spanish nun who undertook a three-year tour of the Holy Lands. Her letter back to her convent led others to travel and visit the shrines in the Holy Land.
Ephesus	Ephesus was an ancient Greek city on the western coat of Asia Minor. It was an important center for early Christianity. The letter to the Ephesians from Apostle Paul is one of the books of the Bible.
Euphrates River	The Euphrates River is in southwestern Asia. It rises in Turkey and flows through Syria and Iraq before joining the Tigris River near the Persian Gulf.

F

Fertile Crescent	This name, the Fertile Crescent, has been given to the area in the Middle East from Israel to the Persian Gulf. The Tigris and Euphrates Rivers are in this area.

G

Gaul	In ancient times, a region in Western Europe was named Gaul. It was invaded and conquered by the Romans.
Georgia	Georgia is an ancient country located on the eastern coast of the Black Sea, bordered by Russia in the north and Turkey and Armenia on the south. It was one of the first countries to accept Christianity.

H

Heraldry	The Crusades led to the beginning of heraldry. Each country had its own emblem and colors. Many different Christian crosses were designed to identify each group that was participating in the battles of the Crusades.
Herod the Great	Herod was born in Palestine and was supported by the Romans. He ruled Judea from 37 BC to 4 BC. He is remembered as a tyrant by the Christians and Jews, for he ordered the massacre of every male baby born in Bethlehem (Matt 2:16).
Hinduism	Hinduism is a religion of India. It is the oldest of the worldwide religions. The Hindus believe in reincarnation.
Holy Land	This name was given to the "Promised Land," especially Galilee and Judea. It is associated with the life of Jesus and the early Christian Church.
Hopi	A group of Native American people of northeastern Arizona are known as the Hopi.

I

Iconoclasts   During the eighth century there was a movement in the Orthodox Church to end the use of icons. The iconoclasts destroyed many icons. This period lasted for one hundred and fifty years.

Indus River   The Indus River rises in Tibet, flows northwest to Kashmir, and then southwest through Pakistan to the Arabian Sea.

Ishmael   The son of Abraham, Ishmael, was expelled into the desert after the birth of his brother Isaac. Muslims regard themselves as descendants of Ishmael.

Isis   In Egyptian mythology, Isis is the goddess of fertility. She was the wife of her brother Osiris, and the mother of Horus.

J

Jerusalem   The ancient city of Jerusalem is home to many sites sacred in the Jewish, Christians, and Islamic traditions.

Jordan River   The Jordan River rises in the Anti-Lebanon Mountains of Lebanon and flows south through the Sea of Galilee and empties into the Dead Sea.

Justinian   Justinian was the Byzantine emperor from 483–565. It was he who codified laws known as the Justinian Code. He is the most illustrious of the early Byzantine emperors. Justinian erected the Church of Holy Wisdom (Hagia Sophia) in Constantinople.

K

Khazars	The Khazars were a principal tribe of the Caucasus.

L

Labarum	The military standard adopted by Emperor Constantine in 312, after his vision of the cross known as the Labarum. It was a banner with the words εν τούτο νίκα (*en touto nika*, "in this sign conquer") with the chi-rho cross. The first two letters of the Greek word for "Christ" (ΧΡΙΣΤΟΣ, *Christos*) are the XP.
Licinius	Licinius was the Roman ruler of the eastern part of the Roman Empire. He cosigned with Constantine the Edict of Milan.
Lintel	The horizontal beam that supports the weight of the wall above a window or a door in called a lintel.
Lombards	In the sixth century, a group of ancient Germanic people, the Lombards, settled in northern Italy.

M

Mesopotamia	The ancient land of Mesopotamia was located between the Tigris and the Euphrates Rivers. It was the site of several early urban civilizations, including Babylonia. The word Mesopotamia means "between two rivers."
Minoan Crete	Minoan Crete was a Bronze Age civilization that flourished in Crete around 3000 BC and 1100 BC.
Monastery of St. Catherine	The Monastery of St. Catherine is located at Mount Sinai and was built by Emperor Jus-

tinian between 527 and 567. This is the site where Moses is supposed to have seen the burning bush. The monastery's library preserves the second-largest collection of codices and manuscripts in the world, outnumbered only by the Vatican Library.

Monophysites	As a group, the monophysites believed that Jesus Christ has a single inseparable nature that is both human and divine.

N

Nero	Nero (37–68), the tyrannical Roman emperor, was deposed by the Senate and then committed suicide. He had persecuted Christians and blamed them for the fire that destroyed Rome in 64.

O

Odin	Odin is the Scandinavian name of the God called "Woden" by the Anglo-Saxons. He was the god of purity, poetry, war, and agriculture.
Osiris	Osiris was one of the chief gods of ancient Egypt. He was the god of death and of afterlife resurrection. Osiris was the brother and husband of Isis.

P

Palatine Hill	The Palatine Hill is one of the Seven Hills of Rome. It is the central hill of the seven and is where the city of Rome was founded.
Passover	The Jewish commemoration of the Exodus, the deliverance of the Israelites from Egypt, is referred to as the Passover.
Pantocrator	Pantocrator is a term for Christ Almighty.

Patriarch	A patriarch is a man who is head of a family or a group. In the Eastern Orthodox Church, the bishops of the sees of Constantinople, Alexandria, Antioch, Jerusalem, Russia, Romania, and Serbia are called Patriarchs.
Persia	Persia was an ancient empire of southwestern Asia. It was at its height during the sixth century BC under the reign of Darius the Great. Alexander the Great conquered Persia in 330 BC.
Phoenicia	Phoenicia was an ancient maritime country west of Syria. Its main cities were Tyre and Sidon.
Pilgrim	A pilgrim is a person who undertakes a journey to a shrine or a sacred place as an act of devotion.
Pope	A person who has authority is referred to as a pope. The head of the Roman Catholic Church, the Bishop of Rome, is the Pope.
Prelate	A high-ranking member of the clergy, such as an abbot or a bishop, is known as a prelate.
Pyrenees	The mountain chain between Spain and France is called the Pyrenees.

R

Rabbi	The leader of a Jewish congregation or the chief religious leader of a synagogue is known as the rabbi.
Ravenna	Ravenna, an ancient Roman city, contains several early Byzantine Christian Churches. It is located in northeastern Italy.
Reliquary	A container or a shrine where relics of a saint are kept is known as a reliquary.

S

Sanskrit

Sanskrit is an ancient Aryan language of the Hindus of India. It is of special interest to philology because it retains many of the supposed characteristics of the parent Indo-European language.

Sarcophagus

An ancient stone or marble coffin often decorated with sculptures and inscriptions is a sarcophagus. The word originally referred to a kind of limestone used for making coffins, in which bodies were thought to decompose quickly. Sarcophagus is from the Greek word for "flesh eater."

Sassanians

The Sassanians were an important dynasty of the Persian Empire.

Steppes

Steppes are an extensive and usually treeless plain. It is often semiarid and grass covered. The vast plains of Russia and the Ukraine are steppes.

Sumer

Sumer was an ancient country of western Asia in northwest Mesopotamia. Archeological discoveries find that the area was settled in 5000 BC. It was prosperous and powerful from 3000 BC until 1700 BC, when it fell into decline and was absorbed into Babylonia and Assyria.

T

Tatar

The Tatars consisted of any one of numerous tribes or hordes, mostly Turkic. They inhabited parts of Russia and western Siberia.

Tiber River

The Tiber River of central Italy rises in the Apennines, flows through Rome, and empties into the Tyrrhenian Sea.

Tigris River	The Tigris River is in southwestern Asia. It rises in southeastern Turkey, flows through Iraq, and then joins the Euphrates River and empties into the Persian Gulf.
True Cross	The True Cross is the actual cross on which Christ was crucified.
Tyre	Tyre was the most important city of the ancient Phoenicians. It is located in southern Lebanon on the Mediterranean Sea.

V

Venus	Venus was the Roman goddess of love and beauty.
Vestal Virgins	In ancient Rome, women tended the sacred fire in the temple of Vesta. Vesta was the goddess of the hearth. There were originally four Vestal Virgins, and later six were added. The women vowed to serve 30 years as Vestal Virgins.

Y

Yemen	Yemen occupies an area on the Arabian Peninsula in southwestern Asia on the Red Sea.
Yucatán Peninsula	The Yucatán Peninsula is located in Central America. In modern times it consists of three Mexican states, Belize, and part of Guatemala.

TIMELINE

Dates BC

5000	Appearance of homes or campsites in Egypt
3030	Appearance of Tau cross in Egypt
3000	Merging of the two kingdoms in Egypt
	Beginning of Minoan civilization
	Mesopotamian city of Ur fell
	Canaanite civilization
2000	Damascus inhabited
	Greek Mid-Bronze Age
1900	New Palace of Troy
1857–1814	Hammurabi Dynasty
1800	Wall built around Jerusalem
1600	Height of Minoan civilization
1500	Migration of Aryans to India

1300	First Assyrian Empire
1200	Dorians invade Greece
	Philistines conquer Canaanites
	Olmec culture on Gulf Coast of Mexico
1100	Decline of Minoan culture
1050	Philistines conquer Hebrews, name the land Palestine
1031	Bronze Age in China
1000	Israelites conquer Canaanites
	Native American Adena culture
753	Founding of Rome
685	Founding of city of Chalcedon
560	Birth of Gautama Buddha
551	Birth of Confucius
539	Babylon falls to the Persians
480	Battle of Salamis
410	Rome falls to the Goths
399	Death of Socrates
356	Birth of Alexander the Great
332	Founding of the city of Alexandria by Alexander the Great
330	Alexander the Great conquers Persia
300	Proto-classic culture in Yucatán
	Native American Hopi culture
297	Celts plunder Delphi
295	Museum and library at Alexandria

206	Han Dynasty in China
200	Greece falls to Rome
	Oaxaca, Mexico has population of 16,000
44	March 15, Caesar murdered by Brutus
37	Herod the Great
4	Herod Antipas tetrarch of Galilee and Peraea
	Birth of Christ

Dates AD

33	Crucifixion of Christ
44	Judea becomes a Roman province
54–68	Persecution of Christians by Nero
64	Execution of St. Paul
79	Destruction of Pompeii and Herculeum by Mt. Vesuvius
First Century	Capital of Eastern Han (China) at Lo Yang
	Moche culture on coast of Peru
135	Hadrian erects temple to Venus over site of True Cross
160?	Birth of Tertullian
200	Six systems of Indian philosophy
235	Persecution of Christians
248	Birth of St. Helena
280	Birth of Constantine
284	Trajus and Diocletian persecute Christians
300	Mayan classic period
303	Persecution of Christians

312	Battle at Milvian Bridge; Constantine's vision of cross
313	Edict of Milan
319	Accession of Chandra Gupta I, founder of Gupta Dynasty in northern India
324	Battle of Chrysopolis; Constantine becomes sole emperor of Roman Empire
325	Constantine enlarges Byzantium, renames it Constantinople
	First Ecumenical Council
335	Consecration of Church of the Holy Resurrection, Jerusalem, after finding of the True Cross
339	Death of Constantine
361	Emperor Julian tries to reinstate paganism
378–395	Theodosius I the Great
381	Second Ecumenical Council
	Egeria travels from Spain to Holy Lands
410	Alaric and Visigoths sack Rome
431	Third Ecumenical Council
451	Fourth Ecumenical Council
532	Justinian erects Church of Holy Wisdom, Constantinople
533	Fifth Ecumenical Council
541	Bubonic plague hits Mediterranean lands
568	Lombards invade Italy
589	Filioque added to Nicene Creed by Synod at Toledo, Spain

610	Heraklios emperor of Byzantine Empire
611	Sassanians take Antioch and Damascus
614	Sassanians take Jerusalem
619	Sassanians take Egypt
627	Heraklios recovers True Cross from Persians, takes it to Constantinople
631	Heraklios returns True Cross to Jerusalem
637	Jerusalem falls to the Arabs
638	Heraklios recovers True Cross, takes it to Constantinople
681	Sixth Ecumenical Council
726	Emperor Leo III removes icon of Christ from Chalke Gate
	Period of Iconoclasm begins
787	Seventh Ecumenical Council
800	Pope Leo III crowns Charlemagne Emperor of the Romans
843	Empress Theodora restores veneration of icons
864	Conversion of Khan Boris of Bulgaria
962	Founding of Great Lavra Monastery at Mt. Athos
987	Conversion of Prince Vladimir of Kiev
1054	Great Schism
1099	First Crusades take Jerusalem
1187	Saladin captures Jerusalem
1202–1204	Fourth Crusade and dispersal of Byzantine treasure to Europe as trophies

BIBLIOGRAPHY

Andreopoulos, Andreas. SIGN OF THE CROSS. Brewster,
    Massachusetts: Paraclete Press, 2006.

Angold, Michael. BYZANTIUM: THE BRIDGE FROM
    ANTIQUITY TO RENAISSANCE. New York: St.
    Martin's Press, 2001.

Bashir, Antony. STUDIES IN THE GREEK ORTHODOX
    CHURCH. n.d.

Benson, George Willard. THE CROSS: ITS HISTORY AND
    SYMBOLISM. New York: Hacker Art Books, 1976; repr.
    2005.

Bruce-Mitford, Miranda. THE ILLUSTRATED BOOK OF
    SIGNS AND SYMBOLS. New York: DK Publishing,
    1996.

Carroll, James. CONSTANTINE'S SWORD. New York:
    Houghton Mifflin, 2002.

Cavarnos, Constantine. ORTHODOX ICONOGRAPHY.
    Belmont, Massachusetts: Institute for Byzantine and
    Modern Studies, 1992.

Cesaeretti, Paolo. THEODORA, EMPRESS OF BYZANTIUM.

New York: Vendome Press, 2004.

Chidester, David. CHRISTIANITY: A GLOBAL HISTORY. San Francisco: Harper, 2002.

CROSS OF MALTA. April 9, 2005. http://www.orderofmalta. org.uk/cross.htm

Cummings, D. THE RUDDER. Chicago, Illinois: Orthodox Christian Educational Society, 1957.

Dersin, Denise. WHAT LIFE WAS LIKE ON THE BANKS OF THE NILE. Alexandria, Virginia: Time-Life Books, 1996.

Ehrman, Burt D. LOST CHRISTIANITIES. New York: Oxford Press, 2003.

Ferguson, George. SIGNS AND SYMBOLS IN CHRISTIAN ART. New York: Oxford University Press, 1958.

Fontana, David. THE SECRET LANGUAGE OF SYMBOLS. San Francisco: Chronicle Books, 1993.

Grant, Michael. CONSTANTINE THE GREAT: THE MAN AND HIS TIMES. New York: Charles Scribner's Sons, 1993.

Haven, Catherine. LITTLE BLACK BOOK. Saginaw, Michigan: Diocese of Saginaw, n.d.

Mango, Cyril. THE EMPIRE OF NEW ROME. New York: Charles Scribner's Sons, 1980.

Mastratonis, George, ed. DIVINE LITURGY OF ST. JOHN CHRYSOSTOM. St. Louis, Missouri: OLOGOS, 1966.

Matthews, Thomas F. BYZANTIUM: FROM ANTIQUITY TO THE RENAISSANCE. New York: Harry N. Abrams, 1998.

Metford, J. C. J. DICTIONARY OF CHRISTIAN LORE AND LEGEND. London: Thames and Hudson, 1983.

Nasser, Seraphim. ORTHODOX PRAYER BOOK. New York: Blackshaw Press, 1938.

Norwich, John Julius. A SHORT HISTORY OF BYZANTIUM. New York: Alfred A. Knopf, 1997.

Orthodox Weekly Bulletin. SIGN OF THE CROSS. Perth Amboy, NJ: Vestal, 1967.

Owasu, Heiki. SYMBOLS OF NATIVE AMERICA. New York: Sterling Publishers, 1999.

Patrinacos, Nicon D. A DICTIONARY OF GREEK ORTHODOXY. Minneapolis: Light and Life, 1984.

Pelikan, Jaroslav. JESUS THROUGH THE CENTURIES. New Haven, CT: Yale University Press, 1985.

Phillips, Jonathan. THE FOURTH CRUSADE. New York: Viking Press, 2004.

Rice, David Talbot. ART OF THE BYZANTINE ERA. New York: Oxford University Press, 1963.

Rubenstein, Richard E. WHEN JESUS BECAME GOD. New York: Harcourt Brace & Company, 1999.

SUN CROSS. November 5, 2005. http://en.wikipedia.org/wiki/Solar_Cross

Troyer, Johannes. THE CROSS AS A SYMBOL AND ORNAMENT. Philadelphia: Westminster Press, 1961.

TRUE CROSS. January 5, 2005. http://en.wikipedia.org/wiki/True_Cross

Ward, Henry Dana. HISTORY OF THE CROSS. London: Nisbet, 1871. Escondido, California: The Book Tree, 1999.

Youngblood, Timothy. July 10, 2005. THE HISTORY OF THE CROSS SYMBOL IN CHRISTIANITY. http://masters_table.org//pagan/cross.htm

Ware, Timothy. THE ORTHODOX CHURCH. New edition. London: Penguin Books, 1997.

WHO WERE THE CELTS? February 17, 2006. http://www.ibilio.org/galic/celts.html

ADDITIONAL READINGS

Carson, Lionel. LIBRARIES OF THE ANCIENT WORLD. New York: Yale University Press, 2001.

CELTIC BRITAINI. February 27, 2006. http://www. britainexpress.com/History/Celtic_Britain.htm

CROSS. Microsoft Encarta 98.1993–1997, Microsoft Corporation.

CRUCIFIX, CROSS. April 9, 2005. http://mb_soft.com/believe/ txn/cross.htm

Freeman, Charles. THE CLOSING OF THE WESTERN MIND. New York: Albert A. Knopf, 2003.

Grant, Michael. A SOCIAL HISTORY OF GREECE AND ROME. New York: Charles Scribner's Sons.

THE ANCIENT MEDITERRANEAN. New York: History Book Club, 1969.

FOUNDER OF THE WESTERN WORLD. New York: Charles Scribner's Sons, 1991.

Koromila, Marianna, THE GREEKS IN THE BLACK SEA. Athens: Panorama, 1991.

Mango, Cyril. THE EMPIRE OF NEW ROME. New York: Charles Scribner's Sons, 1980.

THE OXFORD HISTORY OF BYZANTIUM. New York: Oxford University Press, 2002.

MEDIEVAL SOURCEBOOK. GALARIUS AND CONSTANTINE: EDICTS OF TOLERATION 311/313. March 15, 2006. http://www.fordham.edu/halsall//source/ edict_milan.html>

MEDIEVAL SOURCEBOOK. PROCOPIUS: JUSTINIAN SUPPRESSES THE NIKA REVOLT, 532. May 20, 2004. http://www.fordham.edu/halsall/source/prcop-warsl.html

THE NIKA REVOLT AND COURAGE OF AN EMPRESS. May 20, 2004. http://myroon.sjsu.edu/romeweb/ LATEROME/art13.htm

Norwich, John J. BYZANTIUM: THE DECLINE AND FALL. New York: Alfred A. Knopf, 1996.

Ouspensky, L., and V. Lossky. THE MEANING OF ICONS. Crestwood, New York: St. Vladimir's Press, 1989.

PAGAN CROSSES. July 8, 2005. http://www.assemblyofyhwh.com/pagancrosses.html

Rubenstein, Richard E. ARISTOTLE'S CHILDREN. New York: Harcourt, 2003.

Staniforth, Maxwell, trans. EARLY CHRISTIAN WRITINGS: THE APOSTOLIC FATHERS. St. Ives, England: Clays Ltd., 1968.

Veyne, Paul (ed). A PRIVATE LIFE: FROM PAGAN ROME TO BYZANTIUM. Cambridge, Massachusetts: Belknap Press of Harvard University Press, 1987.

Wells, Colin. SAILING FROM BYZANTIUM. New York: Delacorte Press, 2006.

WHO WAS CONSTANTINE? March 15, 2006. http://home.snu.edu/~dwilliam/f98/milan/history.htm

WALKER METALSSMSITHS. July 8, 2005. http://www.celtsarts.com/celtic.htm